British Naturalists' Association

Guide to
WOODLANDS

Series Editor   Ron Freethy

British Naturalists' Association

Guide to
WOODLANDS

J.L.Cloudsley-Thompson

The Crowood Press

Cover illustrations
Top left: Jay with young
Top right: Silver-washed fritillary
Bottom left: Fly agaric
Bottom right: Badger

To John Sankey

First published by

THE CROWOOD PRESS
Crowood House,
Ramsbury, Marlborough,
Wiltshire SN8 2HE

British Library Cataloguing in Publication Data

Cloudsley-Thompson, J.L.
    The British Naturalists' Association guide to
    woodlands.—(The British Naturalists'
    Association guides; 3)
    1. Forest fauna—Great Britain
    I. Title   II. Series
    574.941   QH137

    ISBN 0-946284-16-4

Design by Vic Giolitto

Set in 10 on 11 point Bembo by
Quadraset Limited, Midsomer Norton, Bath, Avon
Printed in Spain by Graficromo s.a., Cordoba

Contents

Foreword

Since 1905 the British Naturalists' Association has provided opportunities for beginners and more advanced students of natural history to rub shoulders with experts, both amateur and professional.

Throughout this time its magazine, *Country-Side*, and its local, regional and national meetings have fostered the collection and sharing of knowledge concerning the rocks, soils, plants and animals which make up our living landscape. Essential in this process of national learning and the spreading of awareness about wildlife has been the publication of many identification keys – keys to groups like lichens, plant galls, harvestmen and spiders, which though present and often abundant in most habitats were at one time frequently overlooked or wrongly ignored, because there was no way in, no key to unlock the doors of enquiry.

In the same way, the Association's pamphlets entitled 'Let's begin the study of . . .' helped pioneer many branches of field science.

At last, some of that knowledge, the fruit of all those eighty years of unique experience, is now made public in this superb series of books. Habitat by habitat, all is revealed.

Most of my own knowledge of plants and animals was gained in the field by walking with and listening to the 'ologists', the experts in each subject – bryology, ornithology, algology etc, etc. Each trip was an occasion to be remembered thanks to the personal anecdotes and sheer enthusiasm of people who had all the facts at their fingertips and who loved the subject of their expertise.

If you can't go on such trips, these books are the next best thing. Open up the pages and you can almost smell the sweet or rotten smell of a river, see the rooks flying from the beech hangers, and hear the warm buzz of summer insects or the crisp crackle of a winter morning.

If I may be allowed one personal reminiscence. I can remember following John Clegg (the author of the volume on ponds and streams in this series) down to the ponds in the grounds of Haslemere Educational Museum, where he was then curator. *Stratiotes aloides* (water soldier), *Nepa cinerea* (the water scorpion), *Hydrocharis morsus ranae* (frogbit), *Gunnera manicata* (the giant prickly rhubarb from South America). . . . This was the first time I was ever shown these things and I will never forget either the experience or the names.

I am grateful to John Clegg and all the others who led me along the many paths of natural history and to a very full and worthwhile life. I am grateful too to all the officers and members of the British Naturalists' Association, both past and present, for everything they have done and are doing to share their knowledge and wonder of life.

What a super series of books! The only problem is what is the B.N.A. going to do to celebrate its centenary?

David Bellamy

President of the Youth Section of
the British Naturalists' Association
Bedburn, County Durham

 **British Naturalists' Association**

The British Naturalists' Association has existed since 1905, when E. Kay Robinson founded the B.N.A.'s journal *Country-Side* and groups of readers began to hold meetings which gave amateur naturalists an opportunity to meet experts and to discuss topics of mutual interest with them. It is this network of branches all over Britain that forms the basis of the B.N.A. New members are always welcome and enquiries regarding membership should be addressed to Mrs June Pearton, 48 Russell Way, Higham Ferrers, Northamptonshire NN9 8EJ.

During its eighty years of existence many distinguished naturalists and public figures have been associated with the B.N.A. At present the President is Lord Skelmersdale, the President of the Youth Section is David Bellamy, and R.S.R. Fitter, Eric Hosking, Alfred Leutscher, Professor Kenneth Mellanby, Angela Rippon, Sir Peter Scott, Professor Sir Richard Southwood, Sir George Taylor and H.J. Wain are Vice-Presidents of the Association.

Country-Side appears four times a year and publishes articles about every aspect of natural history. Contributions, including photographs and drawings, should be addressed to Ron Freethy, The Editor, *Country-Side*, Thorneyholme Hall, Roughlee, Nr Burnley, Lancashire BB12 9LH.

Author's preface

This volume is not a handbook for the identification of British woodland flora and fauna – there are already many excellent field guides in print to our plants and animals. It is intended for the keen beginner who is starting to develop a more serious interest in natural history and for experienced naturalists, often with specialist knowledge of one or more groups of plants and animals, who have not received much in the way of biological training. The aim of the book is to help bridge the gap between these amateur naturalists and modern professional ecologists.

Much of existing biological knowledge is based on the inspired work of British naturalists during the past century. Unfortunately, today naturalists have little understanding of current ecological ideas, while many ecologists fail to appreciate the valuable work done by naturalists. If by explaining the approach of modern ecologists and forestry workers to the woodland ecosystem this volume helps naturalists to orient their work in a more useful direction, it will have achieved its object.

My warmest thanks are due to Ron Freethy of the British Naturalists' Association for inviting me to write this book and for his invaluable comments; to Dr C. P. Burnham for the use of Figure 6 (first published in *Field Studies*, 5, pp. 349–66); to Dr Ernest Neal, MBE, for Figures 25–27 (redrawn from his book *Woodland Ecology*); to Dr Christopher Perrins for Figure 22 (redrawn from his book *Birds*); to Edward Arnold Ltd for permission to reproduce Figures 29 and 30 (from *Life in the Soil* by R. M. Jackson and F. G. Raw); to Carole Pugh for redrawing Figures 3, 5, 8, 14, 17 and 22–24; and to my wife, Anne Cloudsley, who, as always, has helped me in innumerable ways.

I am also indebted to the various authors on whose diagrams and drawings the following figures are based: H. Godwin (Figures 1 and 2); J. D. Ovington (Figures 3 and 24); A. E. Michaelbacker (Figure 16); B. Seifert (Figure 18); W. S. Bristowe (Figure 15); T. H. Savory (Figure 20); and G. Evans (Figure 28).

J. L. Cloudsley-Thompson

1 The origins of woodlands

Twenty thousand years ago the British Isles and much of Europe were in the grip of the last ice age. Although the southernmost parts of England were not actually covered by sheets of ice, the severe Arctic conditions which prevailed prevented the growth of trees. Only as the climate became milder did the trees return. Later they developed into an almost continuous mantle and as recently as 2,000 years ago large areas of the country were still covered with dense forest. Today, after centuries of deforestation, only fragments remain.

Plant succession

Plants are naturally grouped together into communities whose nature depends upon factors of the environment − such as other plants, climate, soil and animals, including human beings − which interact with one another in numerous ways. The natural vegetation of most of Britain is forest; and if left alone, most of the existing vegetation would eventually revert to woodland. If not subjected to grazing, cutting, burning or ploughing, land now planted with arable crops and grassland would in time be invaded by bushes and eventually by trees. This process is known as 'plant succession', and woodland represents the final stage or 'climax' of the succession in much of Britain.

A primary succession is one starting from bare ground which has not previously had vegetation growing on it or, at least, does not contain any seeds, bulbs, spores or rhizomes that could develop directly into mature plants. Primary successions can be seen on sandbanks cast up by the sea, on bare rock exposed by avalanches, and on newly drained mud-

flats. Any vegetation which appears in such places is the result of immigration. Secondary successions arise in areas which have previously carried vegetation: consequently, they do not have to start quite from the beginning. For example, they may come about when the vegetation has been destroyed by a severe fire, or when a forest has been felled. As a succession progresses, it changes the environment in such a way as to make it less satisfactory for the existing vegetation and more suitable for that of the next stage, or 'sere', which will eventually replace it. The climax vegetation in Britain is usually woodland, except at higher altitudes and in the far north.

The major types of natural climax communities in the British Isles are maritime and coastal vegetation − salt marshes, sand dunes, etc. − aquatic communities, marshes, bogs, grasslands, heaths and moors, mountain communities and woodland. Artificial communities include arable farmland, gardens and orchards, plantations and artificial grasslands.

The natural woodland of Britain is part of the deciduous broad-leaved forest ecosystem which forms the climax vegetation in temperate regions of the northern hemisphere where there is a marked, even if not prolonged, cold season. (Apart from some mountainous districts in the southern Andes of South America and in New Zealand, there is no equivalent in the southern hemisphere.) Leaf-shedding in the temperate zone is an adaptation to the cold season. It takes place even if the trees grow in a greenhouse where they are protected from cold in winter. The factor responsible for initiating the change in colour of leaves in autumn, even before the first frost occurs, is not known for certain, but is probably decreasing day length. It is remarkable that the various species of trees should turn yellow within such a very short period of time (between 10 and 20 October) in central Europe, with no marked distinction between places in the east and in the west.

Evergreen broad-leaved trees are neither resistant to cold nor to the drought caused by freezing of the soil. For this reason, holly trees are not found in central Europe but are restricted to the west. In the cherry laurel photosynthesis – the formation by green plants of organic compounds from water and carbon dioxide using energy absorbed from sunlight – ceases with even the slightest frost. The loss of thin, deciduous leaves in winter and the protection of the buds from water loss results in a saving of material compared with the freezing of thick, evergreen leaves. It is essential, however, that the fresh spring leaves should have a long, warm summer lasting at least four months in which to produce enough reserves for the fruits and buds of the following year. Even bare twigs lose some water by evaporation and in the extreme climate of Siberia the only broad-leaved deciduous trees are those with very small leaves – such as birch, aspen and mountain ash. Where the summers are too cool and too short, deciduous species are replaced by evergreen conifers whose pine needles are resistant to cold and can begin photosynthesis immediately the temperature increases. In this way a short growing season can be exploited to the utmost.

The belt of frost-resistant deciduous forest that forms the climax vegetation of the temperate zone south of the boreal or northern forest and the coniferous forest or 'taiga' biomes consists of many discontinuous populations of trees, separated by long-established barriers of ocean and desert. In both hemispheres, however, closely related species occupy similar ecological niches. The main forest species are oaks, beeches and

pines. Despite their wide distribution and diversity, pines are generally characteristic of coarse, dry soils such as sand, gravel and outcrops of rock. They have deep roots and consequently do not grow well on frozen or poorly drained soils but can withstand hot and dry conditions very well. Oaks, likewise, are deep-rooted trees that occupy dry sites from the southern edge of the boreal forest well into the tropics. In the north temperate zone they are deciduous but, south of the equator, oaks are frequently evergreen. Together with beech, ash and maple, they reach their finest development in the semi-oceanic climate of

Above Oak wood in spring.

Opposite Scots pine discharging clouds of wind-borne pollen.

Left Flower of the larch, a deciduous conifer introduced from Europe in the seventeenth century.

Britain and western Europe, where elm, chestnut, sycamore and lime are also common.

Pollen analysis

In order to understand the complexity of British woodlands, it is necessary not only to study their composition but also to consider where, when, and in what order the species of which they are composed reached the British Isles – for, as we have seen, no trees could have survived the last ice age. The evidence on which the questions can be answered satisfactorily depends to a considerable extent upon the scientific technique of pollen analysis, or 'palynology'. Many deciduous forest trees and all the conifers, are pollinated by wind. Trees of the birch and hazel families bear their inconspicuous flowers in catkins. These are formed in the autumn and mature in spring, when wind pollination takes place – before the production of leaves would hamper the process. Beech and oaks are regularly wind-pollinated, and their flowers are visited only by the insects that collect pollen. Willows and sallows, on the other hand, are frequently visited for their nectar by bees in fine weather, although a considerable amount of pollen is also transferred by the wind.

Wind pollination is obviously advantageous to plants, because it enables them to be independent of insects and can take place when insects are scarce or absent. On the other hand, to be effective, very large amounts of pollen need to be produced and then spread over a distance away from the parent tree's own shade. The stigma of the flower of an oak has an area of about one

square millimetre, and to make pollination reasonably certain about one million pollen grains have to be deposited on every square metre of the tree's habitat. It is not surprising, therefore, that pollen grains should rain down throughout the British Isles continuously from February to the end of September – although tree pollen is most common early in the year whereas pollen from grasses, nettles and plantains dominates in the autumn. The pollen grains of wind-pollinated plants usually have a smooth, dry surface so that they are dispersed singly or in twos and threes and do not stick together in clumps (as do the sticky, ornamented grains of flowers that are pollinated by insects).

Most of the pollen grains that fall to the earth rot and disappear. Some, however, fall into lakes or waterlogged fens and peat bogs where, in the absence of oxygen, the living contents of the grains disappear while their outer membranes are preserved for hundreds of thousands of years. Pollen grains from different species of tree are easily recognisable when examined under the microscope, even after preservation (see Figure 1). Because they are resistant to severe chemical treatment,

Figure 1 Pollen grains of British trees and shrubs commonly preserved in mud and peat. (The scale is one tenth of a millimetre in length.)

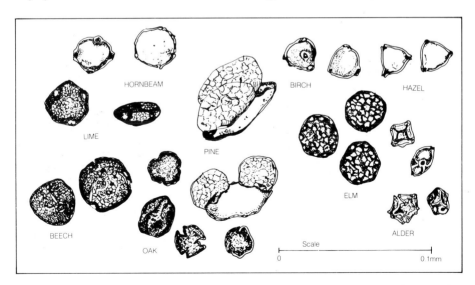

pollen grains can be separated from peat or mud at various depths, and analysed. Comparing changes in the different types of pollen throughout a series of samples gives an indication of the changes which have taken place in the vegetation. Within each sample, some 150 tree pollen grains are counted, and each species represented as a percentage of the total. The pollen of hazel and of herbaceous plants – non-arboreal pollen – is also usually expressed as a percentage of the arboreal pollen, although not reckoned in the total.

In any one example, changes in plant succession are indicated by the differing percentage of pollen grains of the various species of trees at different depths for, in a pollen diagram (Figure 2), greater depth in the sample indicates a greater age. Although the pollen of certain trees, such as rowan, yew and apple, is not preserved well, the pollen grains of many important forest trees are preserved, and pollen analysis can yield a reasonably reliable and complete history of Britain's former forests.

Since the retreat of the glaciers began at the end of the last ice age, some 20,000 years ago, the vegetation of the British Isles has under-

gone a series of changes. Pollen diagrams and fossil plants indicate that the first vegetation to colonise the newly exposed land surface was tundra, dominated by sedges and grasses, with dwarf birch and arctic willows in abundance. This open landscape was the home of large grazing herbivores such as the giant Irish elk, reindeer and, possibly, bison and wild horses. Mammoths, too, may have roamed the countryside then, hunted by the last of the Old Stone Age people who were beginning to cross over from the continent of Europe. As the climate improved, trees such as aspen, birches and pine spread and dominated the vegetation for a while. Then the cold returned, and the woodland disappeared

Figure 2 A typical pollen diagram through the deposits of Hockham Mere, a deep drained lake in Norfolk. It covers a very large part of late-glacial and post-glacial time, and upon examination the changing proportions of the different tree pollens from base to top will be seen to indicate the general drift of forest history described in the text. The latest phase of reversion of woodland history is only weakly shown at this site. (The figures on the left indicate distance from the surface of the lake deposits down to the sand of the lake basin.)

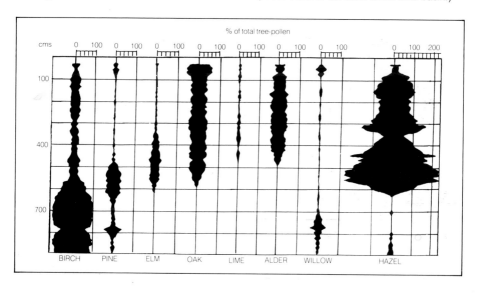

Above Dogwood, a common woodland undershrub.

Opposite (top) Beech wood in spring.

Opposite (bottom) Beech wood in autumn.

Below The poisonous berries of black bryony, a climbing plant of hedges and woods.

– to be replaced, once more, by tundra vegetation.

The post-glacial period began some 10,500 years ago, with a rapid recession of the remaining ice sheets and the development of woodlands. The countryside was covered with open birch forest, while favoured localities in the south supported pine with traces of oak, hazel and elm. It is still not known whether such trees, which require a comparatively warm climate, immigrated from Europe across the dry bed of the North Sea or whether they survived on land lying to the south of our present coastline, and which subsequently became submerged.

As the climate improved, birch was replaced by pine, and the amount of hazel pollen in the air was greater than it has ever been before or since, especially in the west of the country. At the same time, elm, oak and lime became established as important constituents of the lowland forests of England. Lime was absent from Ireland, however, and, like beech and hornbeam, was never a natural forest tree there during the post-glacial period. In contrast, elm was particularly abundant in Ireland. Next came oak and small quantities of alder, while pine retained its hold in many places – for mixed oak forest was not yet dominant everywhere. These conditions persisted for some 2,000 years during the so-called Boreal period, during which the Baltic was a freshwater lake and the North Sea expanded to its present limits. Mesolithic man fished and hunted with wooden spears and arrows tipped with sharp flints, and with weapons made from bone and the antlers of deer. The larger mammals became extinct when the open pastures were replaced by continuous dense woodland.

By the end of the Boreal period, some 8,500 years ago, the climate had become even warmer; pine trees declined and mixed oak forests established complete dominance. At the beginning of the Iron Age, about 6,000 years later, however, a profound climatic deterioration influenced western Europe. Bogs and quagmires appeared while at higher altitudes and in the west the forests were overwhelmed with deep blankets of peat. Birch again became the dominant tree, and there was a southward movement of the vegetational belts. Lime became less frequent, while the numbers of beech and hornbeam trees increased. At the dawn of historical times, British forests were dominated by

Deciduous woodland in winter.

Silver birches, southern England.

alder, elm, oak, birch and beech trees. Until then, forests had been the natural climax vegetation. After the time of the Roman conquest, however, instead of dominating the human population of the land, the forests themselves succumbed to destruction by man so that at the present time only a few remnants persist to remind us of their former glories.

The destruction of the natural forests and the creation of grasslands began on chalk soils during Neolithic times, the extent of the cleared areas increasing slowly and irregularly. In the Roman period there were still large forests in southern England and the Midlands and, further north and in Ireland, the forests were virtually intact. The main changes began with the coming of the Saxons in the fifth century. A thousand years later, there was a great shortage of timber in Britain and by the seventeenth century only 16 per cent of the country was still wooded. The present figure is less than 5 per cent. Destruction of the woodland habitat has resulted in the local extinction of most of the kinds of animals that once inhabited it. Even so, remnants of our woodlands are fortunately still sufficiently numerous and widely distributed to enable the majority of animal species to survive somewhere or other in the British Isles.

Carbon-14 dating

The majority of British woodland trees are wind-pollinated, as are grasses and sedges. When they flower in early summer, clouds of pollen, blowing like yellow smoke, are a familiar sight. Most wind-pollinated plants have mechanisms which prevent the release of pollen under calm and windless conditions. Pollen may be released both at night and during the day – as sufferers from hay fever are only too well aware. Not only are huge amounts of pollen deposited – counts of over 5,000 grains per square centimetre per year have been recorded – but the grains may be carried in the air for long distances before they finally settle on the ground. A piece of mud, no larger than a pip, can easily contain several hundred pollen grains. Some of these may be of local origin, while others may have come from far away. The position of the deposits, too, may be secondary, especially in the case of mineral sediments. Boulder clays containing pollen grains are sometimes derived from other inter-glacial beds, and so on.

Another major problem is to date the pollen samples accurately. If the pollen is in a portion of mud or clay attached to a flint tool or potsherd, for instance, positive dating may be obtained from this. Wherever possible, conclusions reached through pollen analysis must be confirmed by radiocarbon dating, since only this provides an accurate time-scale. The isotope carbon-14, some of which occurs in atmospheric carbon dioxide, can be used for dating organic materials. On their death, plants cease to photosynthesise, and do not take up any more carbon-14 from the air. That already taken up undergoes radioactive decay (the rate of which is known) to become normal carbon-12. It is, therefore, possible to determine how long has elapsed since the death of a plant by measuring the amount of radioactive carbon-14 still remaining in its tissues. The dating of pollen samples, hitherto a matter of inspired guesswork based on comparison with similar samples from other localities, can today be confirmed by radiocarbon analysis of fragments of wood, bone and other materials.

Much of the impetus behind the early development of palynology stemmed from the fact that it offered a dating system for the period between the last glaciation and the present. Accordingly, events during this period were dated by reference to the classic pollen zones of the British Isles. More recently, however, radiocarbon dating has progressively been used to confirm the age of material containing pollen grains.

Apart from information gained through the analysis of pollen samples from peat bogs and through radiocarbon dating, evidence for the post-glacial history of the British flora is

Birch wood with bracken, Loch Lomond.

somewhat scanty. There is little doubt, however, that the south-eastern corner of England was joined to the continent of Europe for one or two thousand years after the final disappearance of the ice sheets. The raising of the sea levels and land subsidence which later formed the Straits of Dover began about 8,000 years ago. A narrow passage linked the North Sea with the English Channel for a period of several thousand years after this, but then submergence was resumed and the shores retreated to their present positions. Although the Straits of Dover are still rather narrow, they have not only slowed the return to Britain of many plant and animal species from the continental mainland, but have excluded others altogether. In a similar way, the Irish Sea, rather than St Patrick, has probably been responsible for the absence of snakes from Ireland. Although different ecological conditions probably account for many absences, only 67·5 per cent of the plant species found in Great Britain inhabit Ireland today.

Coppiced woodland, with old pollarded hornbeam.

Evidence of the rising water level and of land subsidence that has taken place around the British coast is provided by the presence of submerged forests in a number of places. These are sometimes known as 'Noah's Woods' from a popular myth that they were drowned at the time of the Biblical deluge. Their positions, near the extreme low tide mark, suggests that these forests represent the last general phase of submergence – which may not yet have ended. Indeed, on the coast of Dorset, subsidence is apparently still proceeding.

The origins of animals

Although a few species of animals have evolved in the British Isles and later spread to the Continent, the majority developed abroad and came to these islands after the last of the Pleistocene ice ages. Except for a few conspicuous species which were introduced in historic times and whose modes of arrival and establishment have been recorded, the way the various species arrived is unknown. Probably many of them came by several different routes at the same time. Some animals arrived under their own powers of locomotion; others were carried by air, sea, or on the bodies of other animals. The species that arrived by the sea were probably carried on driftwood and other floating debris, or were imported, either deliberately or accidentally, by man. Such introductions include the rabbit, which became established in the thirteenth century and has greatly affected the vegetation and, consequently, the relative abundance of other animal species, and the grey squirrel, which has spread over the country, replacing the native red squirrel in many places. More recent importations include the muskrat, mink and coypu, which have escaped from fur farms. The muskrat was exterminated with some difficulty, but mink and coypu are now firmly established.

Most of the terrestrial vertebrates of the British Isles migrated overland from the

Above The stalkless acorn cups of the Turkey oak, covered with mossy scales.

Right Beech nuts, whose seeds or 'mast' are an important food of woodland animals.

Below Holly seedlings emerging through a carpet of oak leaves.

continent of Europe. At various times since the retreat of the glaciers there were land connections which made this possible. Subsequent extinctions, caused by climatic deterioration, may account for the absence from Ireland of a number of animals. Some, like the natterjack toad and pearl-bordered fritillary butterfly, have very restricted ranges in

Larch and pine, with underlying beech.

ranges in Ireland than they do at present. If they have become extinct over the greater part of their original ranges in Ireland, it is quite possible that yet other species may have become completely extinct in that country. That, and not inability to cross the land connections, could perhaps explain the absence of adders and slow worms from Ireland. It is not yet known which is the true explanation. This may also explain the absence of the black grouse, tawny owl, toad, palmate newt and certain insects. The grass snake and smooth snake never spread sufficiently far north to reach the land connection. The complete destruction of pine by humans in Ireland may have caused the disappearance of such conifer-inhabiting species as the great spotted woodpecker, crossbill and crested tit.

The British fauna may, therefore, include the descendants of two or more populations of animals that invaded these islands after different ice ages, and which may have subsequently interbred; while the reduced fauna and flora of the offshore islands could be accounted for by a number of explanations – the absence of land connections after the last glacial period, immigrations and subsequent extinctions, and the inability of comparatively small land areas to support large numbers of species of plants and animals.

Man is believed to have entered Britain during Upper Palaeolithic times, as the ice sheets melted, and lived at first by hunting, fishing and gathering edible plants to eat. Stock raising and agriculture began about 2400 BC, by which time the vegetation had somewhat recovered from the devastation caused by the Pleistocene glaciations. As we have already seen, the British woodlands remained relatively intact until the arrival of the Saxons in the fifth century AD.

Ireland but in England, Scotland and Wales, although local, have ranges that cover the greater part of the country. At some time in the past, therefore, they probably had wider

2 Types of woodlands

The deciduous summer forest formation of western and central Europe is the climax vegetation of the plains, valleys and lower hill slopes of England, Wales and much of Scotland and Ireland. The dominant trees are oaks, with beech on chalk and limestone in the south of England. In northern localities, beyond the area of the beech, calcareous soils are dominated by ash woods – although these are seldom very large. Ash pollen predominates in the fossil record only after widespread disturbance of the forest by Neolithic man had taken place.

Other British trees, which may be dominant locally in widely distributed communities, are the alder, birch, hornbeam and yew. Indeed, on the chalk of the South Downs, yew may well be the climax dominant. In general, however, the trees are usually co-dominants in the 'society'; hornbeam tends to be subordinate to the oaks, the yew to beech and sometimes, also, to oak. There is, today, very little woodland left untouched by human activity, except perhaps in some remote valleys and towards the upper limits of the forest.

The oak woods thin out in northern Scotland. In the far north and central regions, where the climate differs distinctly from that of the rest of the British Isles, there are natural woods of Scots pine and widespread forests of birch. These Caledonian pine and birch associations belong to a completely different formation from the deciduous forests to the south, and represent part of the coniferous forest belt of northern Europe.

Virgin forest is thus rare in the British Isles, except in the more remote mountainous regions. Most of the woodland has been selectively felled for centuries, which has altered its composition and sometimes its whole character. Opening the canopy, which lets in more light, kills some woodland plants and promotes the growth of others. It also enables herbs and grasses, which cannot grow at all in deep shade, to make their appearance and to overshadow the true shade plants of the woodland floor. In this way, the ground vegetation may be completely changed.

Plantations of native trees, if left to themselves, develop into communities almost indistinguishable from natural woodland. In many places, however, exotic trees such as spruce, pine and larch have been planted. These develop artificial communities with ground vegetation completely different from that of Britain's natural woods. They are sometimes invaded by woodland herbs which manage to establish themselves; more often, the soil remains virtually bare.

Oak woods

Deciduous oak forest is the natural climax vegetation over a large part of the British Isles, except on the most sterile sands, shallow limestone, permanently wet soils, and places constantly exposed to violent winds – below an altitude of 300–450m (1,000–1,500ft). This is confirmed by analysis of the pollen content of peat bogs, fossilised remains of old forests and, since Roman times, by documentary evidence. The scattered remains of more or less natural oak woods point to the same conclusion. Many British oak woods are, today, coppice with standards. They contain a layer of shrubs, usually hazel, which is, or ought to be, cut at intervals of from 8 to 12 years, so that branches shoot up again from

Above Young bracken fronds

Right The rare oxlip

the cut stocks. The tall oaks are themselves spaced so that their crowns scarcely meet. Beneath the topmost stratum there is often another layer of shorter trees – either younger oaks or subordinate species – and beneath this an undergrowth of shrubs. The layer of herbs in a wood is termed the 'field layer', while growing close to the soil there may also be a layer of mosses or lichens. A soft-grass, bracken and bluebell society is commonly seen in open oak woods where the soil is shallow. These three herbs can live very close to one another without competing: their roots and underground parts lie at different levels, while their aerial shoots mature at different seasons of the year. On deeper soils, however, bracken rhizomes may compete with bluebell

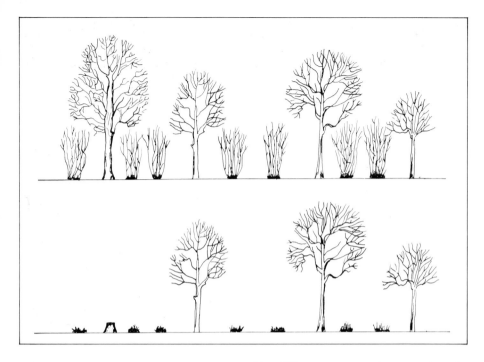

Figure 3 Coppice with standards system of woodland management. Above, before felling; below, after felling with one standard tree felled.

bulbs. The naturalist studying woodland vegetation will pay particular attention to the stratification or layering of the vegetation.

Coppice with standards (Figure 3) has been the traditional form of exploited oak wood in the English lowlands for centuries and in the past was often planted on open ground. This man-made type of woodland has also been formed from the original oak forests, where hazel was the dominant shrub in the undergrowth. Most of the younger trees were cut out so that those which remained were able to spread and, when mature, their outermost twigs just touched those of neighbouring trees. The curved timber of the heavy main branches, developed under these conditions, was especially useful for building wooden ships. When trees grow closer together, the canopy is dense and their crowns are narrow at the top. The open canopy of regularly exploited oak wood allows plenty of light to reach the shrub layer, promoting continuous growth which was, and sometimes still is, harvested for fences, hurdles, bean poles, and so on.

With the disappearance of wooden ships, the spreading oaks of old England lost their value. Many of the remaining oak woods are now neglected: felled and dead trees are no longer replaced, and the coppice is not cut regularly. Some woods are used merely as preserves for pheasants or as fox coverts, a few as nature reserves.

There are two species of mature oak in Britain: the common or pedunculate, and the durmast or sessile oak. The common oak bears acorns on long, slender stalks while in the durmast the acorns are either without a stalk or with only a short, thick one. There are also

Above Primroses and lesser celandine

Left Late spider orchid

minor differences in the shape of the leaves, those of the sessile oak having longer stalks. The common oak is the familiar species of the southern, eastern and midlands woods; the durmast, of the west and north. It also occurs, either alone or in mixed communities, with the common oak, on sandy soils in south-eastern England. The two are similar in general appearance and hybridise readily when they grow together. (Three other species of oak have been introduced into the British Isles, but they do not form a component of our woodlands. They are the Mediterranean, holm or evergreen oak, the Turkey oak, which has recently spread into some northern woodlands, and the American red oak.)

The dominant trees of British woodlands,

common and sessile oaks, are frequently associated with ash, hornbeam, birch, wych elm, aspen, maple, alder and gean or wild cherry. The second layer of trees, when present, may contain rowan or mountain ash, holly, service tree and crab apple. All these subsidiary trees may be coppiced. The shrub layer is often dense. While hazel is the most common shrub, especially in the south, hawthorn, blackthorn, dogwood, elder, willow and guelder-rose are also sometimes found.

In the sessile oak woods of south-western England, hornbeam is a coppiced shrub, while hawthorns, willows and brambles are common, holly, guelder-rose, alder, buckthorn and service tree less frequent. The field layer is somewhat scanty, although bramble and bracken societies may be well developed.

Right Toothwort

Below Herb Paris

Dog's mercury, with a sedge growing through.

Mosses, liverworts and lichens are particularly common in woods growing in the damper climate of the west.

Periodic cutting of the coppice has a pronounced effect on the vegetation of the floor of a wood. The sudden increase in light intensity stimulates the growth and flowering of the herbs so that, after two or three years, the ground is covered with sheets of lovely primroses, wood anemones, violets and blue-bells. As the shrubs grow up, however, and their canopy closes in, the herbaceous vegetation becomes sparse and many of the plants cease to flower.

After the spring-flowering species have bloomed the beauty of oak woods is enhanced by species which flower later during the year. These include wood sorrel, dog's mercury, foxglove, wood sanicle, St John's wort, herb Robert, enchanter's nightshade, wood avens,

and many others. Where there is loose soil or decaying organic debris, clumps of stinging nettles may be found, often so dense that other herbs are excluded. Moss and fungi are generally abundant, the latter usually producing their conspicuous toadstools and spore-bearing reproductive structures in the autumn. Bugle appears on damp, heavy soil, while bracken forms extensive societies to the exclusion of other species where the ground is drier. Its green fronds shade the soil so densely that shorter plants cannot compete with it. Furthermore, its underground rhizomes are frequently matted together so thickly that there is little space for anything else to grow, while the dead and decaying fronds make the earth unsuitable for the establishment of other plant species.

Four main types of oak wood can be distinguished:

1 Oak woods on well aerated clays and loams with a medium water content. The

Solomon's seal

Wood anemones

trees are generally well grown and the dominant hazel is accompanied by a variety of other shrubs. There is a rich field layer.

2   Oak woods on drier, more acid soil. There are fewer shrubs in these, and the field layer contains fewer species. Bracken fern is prominent, associated with bluebells and softgrass, foxgloves, wood sage and St John's wort.

3   Oak woods on very acid sands. Here the trees are often stunted; there is an abundance of birch but very few undershrubs. The field layer consists of bilberry, heather, heath grasses and heath bedstraw.

4   Oak woods on heavy clay which is waterlogged or very wet in winter. These often have an abundance of alder and sallow. The field layer contains tufted hair-grass, rushes, sedges, nettles and creeping buttercup.

Beech woods

Beech woods have a much more restricted distribution in Britain than oak woods, although they are found extensively on the chalk of the North and South Downs, the Chiltern Hills, Dorset, Wiltshire, the Wye Valley and the Cotswolds – where they have been preserved for making furniture. Beech is intolerant of waterlogged soils, but competes successfully with oak on chalk. Although concentrated on limestone soils, forming woods known as 'hangers' on chalk slopes, the finest beeches grow on deep loams overlying chalk plateaux and not at all calcareous. Beech trees are also found on acid sands and gravels in Epping Forest, Burnham Beeches, and in many places around the Weald. They are occasionally associated with ash and gean; yew and holly sometimes form a second tier.

The beech is one of the most strikingly beautiful of British trees. The smooth grey trunks support a canopy of leaves. These change from a delicate green in the spring to a darker hue in high summer and, in autumn, to a glorious bronze. The foliage clothing the spreading branches is so dense that little light penetrates the canopy. Consequently, the undergrowth and field layers are sparse or absent. The emptiness of beech woods results in long vistas, while the thick, persistent carpet of warm brown leaf litter, which appears purple when soaked by the winter rains, confers a singular beauty on the woodland scene.

The deep leaf litter and mould is associated with the development of many superficial roots bearing numerous 'mycorrhiza'. These are shortened roots, covered with symbiotic fungal threads or 'hyphae'. They can be seen easily if the dead leaves that cover them are scraped away. Although it has sometimes been suggested that mycorrhiza are merely examples of limited parasitic attacks, the establishment of beech seedlings appears to be dependent upon the presence of mycorrhizal fungi, which supply an essential trace element. In dense beech woods, mycorrhizal plants and 'saprophytes' – plants living on dead organic matter – may be the only herbs. Among saprophytes characteristic of beech woods are the birdsnest orchid and yellow birdsnest (which is not an orchid), while mycorrhizal plants are represented by the helleborines and the twayblade orchid. Where the woods are more open, and in clearings, a denser field layer is found, containing wood violets, wild strawberries, dog's mercury, cuckoo-pint, sweet woodruff, wood sanicle,

Wild gladiolus under bracken, New Forest.

enchanter's nightshade, bugle, wood sedge and a number of woodland grasses. A ground layer of mosses, liverworts and fungi is characteristic.

Three main types of beech wood, depending upon differences of soil, can be distinguished:

1 The 'hangers' of chalk escarpments and valley sides. The ground is covered with leaf litter, except on steep or windy slopes. The litter is gradually converted into black humus, below which is a layer of highly calcareous mineral soil overlying the weathered surface of the chalk rock, which is reached at a depth of about half a metre. The humus and mineral soil are filled with the fine branches of the surface beech roots and their associated

Left Early purple orchid

Opposite Cuckoo-pint, with berries

Below Guelder rose

mycorrhiza, which not only play a part in nutrition but also anchor the roots down into fissures of the chalk. In summer, the soil becomes very dry, which is an important cause of the frequent sparseness of leaf litter. Common dominants of the field layer are dog's mercury and wood sanicle. Creeping ivy often covers the ground and the trunks of the trees. Flowers especially characteristic of chalk beech woods include hairy violet, sweet woodruff, wall lettuce and melie-grass. Less common are columbine, green hellebore, Solomon's seal, spurge laurel and orchids – helleborines, the birdsnest orchid and its fellow saprophyte, the yellow birdsnest. Mosses may be numerous, but the moss layer

is never continuous.
2 Beech woods on deep loam. Here the leaf litter persists to a depth of several centimetres and there is a dearth of shrubs. Oaks may be frequent locally, although they are dominated by the beeches, which cast a deeper shade and equal the oak in height. Where the canopy is not too dense, the field layer is dominated by brambles and wood sorrel.
3 Beech woods on acid sands and gravels. The trees are often short and crooked where the fertility of the soil is low. The beeches are sometimes accompanied by oaks, rowans and birches. Alder, buckthorn, sallow and holly are characteristic shrubs; hazel, maple and ash are absent. When present, the field layer may

Above Sweet violets, white variety.

Left Sneezewort, a plant of marshy clearings.

contain bracken, bilberry, heather and soft-grasses. The floor of the wood is covered with leaf litter with a discontinuous layer of mosses.

Ash woods

Ash is abundant throughout the British Isles, and is common in woods that are dominated by other trees. It is frequently a dominant itself in a successional stage leading to beech woods, and is the climax dominant on some calcareous soils, especially in the north and west of the country. Limestone ash woods are well developed in the Derbyshire dales, West Yorkshire, Wales, and the Mendip and

Cotswold Hills. Trees which accompany the ash include aspen, wych elm, whitebeam, yew and maple. Ash casts a much lighter shade than the oaks, and a rich undergrowth of shrubs – including hazel, spindle-tree, hawthorn, buckthorn, privet,' dogwood, willows, roses and brambles – is often developed. The field layer has a rich flora too, depending on the amount of water in the soil. Lesser celandine and ransoms are often dominant on damper soils; on drier ground, dog's mercury, often with moschatel and ground ivy, is frequently abundant. Mosses and liverworts are common.

Alder woods

From the abundance of pollen grains preserved in peat, it is evident that woodland dominated by the common alder has been very extensive since mid-glacial times, but has been considerably reduced in extent with the drainage of wet, low-lying land in recent centuries. The largest areas of alder now existing are to be found in East Anglia, where the alder dominates other trees in many fen woods and along the edges of some of the Broads. Elsewhere, alder grows in water-logged soil if it is not too acid, associated with birch, crack willow and ash. Alder is able to thrive in marshy conditions where the soil lacks nitrogen, because its roots form an association with bacteria which utilise nitrogen from the atmosphere. Sallow, guelder-rose, buckthorn, hawthorn, spindle and privet are common shrubs of alder woods, while the herb layer is largely composed of marsh plants such as sedges, marsh marigold, meadowsweet, fen fern, yellow flag, comfrey, stinging nettle, red and yellow loosestrife. Mosses and liverworts are abundant.

Yew woods

Yews are frequent in some types of beech wood, and occasionally form pure stands, as on the North and South Downs. In such

Cuckoo-pint: spathe and spadix.

cases, the yews cast such deep shade throughout the year that most, if not all, other plants are suppressed. The foliage of yew is poisonous, as are the seeds and the thin brown flaking bark. Thrushes and other birds are able to eat the fruit because they do not digest the seeds. Yews are common in country churchyards; according to tradition the first Christian missionaries to Britain sheltered beneath their evergreen branches. The yew is also a symbol of life and its leaves were once scattered on graves. The longbows of medieval archers were cut from knot-free lengths of tall, carefully selected trees.

Birch woods

Birch woods are common on sandy and

Tansy, common on the edges of woods.

gravelly heaths in southern England. The silver birch and the hairy birch, with its browner bark, are common throughout the British Isles on both wet and dry soil except on limestone. Some birch woods are relics of oak–birch forest from which the oaks have been removed. Frequently they represent stages in the secondary succession leading to oak–birch heath or oak woods. Birches are important dominant trees in northern England and in Scotland, where they form the upper limit of forest in the mountains of Inverness and Perthshire at about 600m (2,000ft). Rowan is the principal tree accompanying birch, and there are rather few undershrubs. The field layer in close birch wood consists largely of oak seedlings but in more open woods is composed mainly of plants from the surrounding moorland, including heather, bilberry and grasses.

The razor strop is a common bracket fungus on birch trees. As its name suggests, it was once used for stropping razors. The fruiting body first appears as a white knob which expands into a bracket that is pale brown above and white beneath. The underside is perforated by fine pores through which the spores are liberated. The timber of the trees on which this fungus grows becomes reduced to a brown crumbling state as the tree dies. Sometimes tiers of brackets grow from a single diseased tree.

Pine woods

British pine woods fall into at least two distinct groups: primitive woods of Scots pine derived from the northern coniferous forest, and the remnants of post-glacial forests of southern pine which were greatly added to and extended by planting during the seventeenth and eighteenth centuries. On light, sandy soils in Hampshire, Sussex, Surrey and Kent, pine woods established themselves spontaneously in some places. However, many were cleared during the two world wars for use as pit props. Pine grows naturally on the same sandy soils as birch, and the two trees are frequently seen together. The Scottish pine woods are but scattered remains of formerly extensive forests, and the density of tree growth within them varies considerably. In the south of England pine rejuvenates naturally, and stages in succession leading to tall pine wood can be seen in many places.

Pine trees cast deep shade, and the ground beneath them is often almost bare, carpeted only with a thick layer of slowly decaying pine needles. Species of wintergreen and certain orchids, such as the lesser twayblade and coral-root, are rare species of the Scottish pine forests. In more open pine wood, there may be a scanty field layer of ferns and bracken, bilberry or cowberry, and heather. Mosses are often abundant and, in some pine woods, bog mosses form an important element of the ground flora. In the autumn, a rich fungal flora develops.

In addition to the natural differences between coniferous and deciduous forests, most intensively managed conifer plantations are highly artificial. The trees are usually uniform in age, species and spacing, and so lack variety. They are cropped rather than being left to die, so that there is an absence of rotten wood to provide living conditions for wood-boring insects, and for any basis for food chains to develop. Furthermore, coniferous trees are, for economic reasons, often planted in poor soil and on exposed hillsides which, in any case, are not conducive to a rich flora and fauna. Fortunately for the naturalist, the average coniferous forest contains stands of trees in different stages of growth. In addition, it is broken up by a network of roads and rides through which timber is extracted. These create biologically rich habitats on the verge of the forest, while plants such as foxgloves and willow-herb thrive on the disturbed soil.

As a whole, British woodlands are semi-natural – apart from modern plantations of conifers. That is, they are more or less modified descendants of the original natural forest. In the south, both oak and beech woods have largely been planted, probably often in places where these trees were formerly dominant. Some beech woods, however, and many oak woods are the direct descendants of natural forest – but conditions have been altered so drastically that, today, the natural regeneration of oak and beech occurs only occasionally. Ash reproduces more abundantly, and distributes its fruits more widely, than either oak or beech and, consequently, more often springs from seed. The same is true of the birches, which require well lit surroundings and are unable to grow effectively in competition with oak or beech.

3 Woodland soils

Soil is the superficial covering of the earth's crust, which is weathered by physical, chemical and biotic influences to form distinct layers, or 'horizons'. British soils today are not, however, necessarily related to the rocks above which they lie. As the glaciers of the ice age moved slowly along, they carved out deep valleys, ground down the rocks beneath them, and transported boulders, stones and earth from one place to another. As the ice finally melted, the water and rain sorted out the particles, leaving the soil much as it is today but with little organic content and often far removed from its parent rocks.

In its solid phase, soil has two main constituents: mineral material, ultimately derived by weathering of the rocks, and organic matter. Both these components are produced by decomposition or transformation. In the case of parent rocks, these agents are mainly physico-chemical, although living organisms also play a part in the process, while the decomposition of organic litter is predominantly influenced by soil organisms, physical and chemical agents being less important in this process. Mature soil results from the integration of mineral and organic matter, its structure and texture as well as its alkalinity or acidity being determined at the same time. When removed from their parent rocks, soils are said to be 'derived'; and when transported from other areas by rivers and deposited in valleys, they are usually referred to as 'alluvial' soils.

Soil formation

Naturalists strolling through a lovely wood and enjoying the birds, butterflies or wild flowers may well be excused if they forget the earth beneath their feet. Yet the woodland vegetation and its associated fauna are entirely dependent upon climate and soil – the latter produced by the weathering of the parent rocks that make up the earth's crust. Weathering is achieved by a combination of three processes.

Physical weathering Rock is broken up by heating and cooling. This, and especially the action of frost, causes expansion and contraction of the minerals in the parent material, separating them into individual particles. Physical disintegration is also caused by wetting and drying, percolating water removing the particles mechanically.

Chemical weathering This can take several forms, one of which is hydration – the addition of water to one of the chemical constituents of the parent rock to form a new compound. An example is the hydration of hematite (oxide of iron) into a series of related minerals (which vary according to the amount of water combined with the hematite). This process causes expansion of the minerals, and so helps to disintegrate the rock. Hydrolysis also involves the chemical reaction of a mineral with water. The process is more complicated than hydration and results in the formation of entirely new compounds. Oxidation is an important stage in the weathering of many rocks once air and water have been admitted into the interstices. Reduction is the reverse of oxidation, and occurs when there is a deficiency of oxygen, as in waterlogged areas or when much decaying vegetation is present, in bogs and marshes. Finally, rocks may be weathered chemically by carbonation. When atmospheric carbon dioxide dissolves in rainwater, a weak solution of carbonic acid is formed which tends to dissolve alkaline or 'basic' rocks. Carbon dioxide is also taken up in soil water from organic matter produced during the decomposition of plant and animal remains. Limestones, chalk and basic soils are particularly susceptible to carbonation. Removal of their calcareous components causes some rocks to disintegrate. Chemical changes are usually more drastic than physical weathering, producing new minerals, often in very small crystals – notably hydrated ferric oxide and clay minerals. The resulting soil horizons are often of a brighter brown or yellow in colour than their parent material.

Biotic weathering Once weathering has begun, the wedging action of roots, especially along the boundaries of particles and grains and in natural weaknesses such as faults and joints, helps to disintegrate the parent materials from which the soil has been derived. Root tips secrete various chemicals, some of which are acidic and dissolve the basic minerals with which they come into contact. Bacteria and fungi, responsible for the decomposition and decay of dead plants and animals, make an important contribution to carbonation and chemical weathering. Burrowing animals, such as earthworms, moles, rabbits and badgers, help to break up the overlying soil, enabling air, water and the products of decay to penetrate right down to the parent rock, where weathering is taking place all the time.

Throughout the lowlands of Britain, soil particles have suffered so many changes over such a long period of time that only the most resistant have been able to survive as sand or silt. Sand grains are from about 0·02 to 2·0mm in diameter, while silt particles lie between 0·002 and 0·02mm in diameter. Those capable of decomposition have been weathered to even smaller dimensions. In

Above Yellow stereum
Below Many-zoned polypore

consequence, although the parent rocks contain on average only about 12 per cent of quartz, the sand and silt fractions of lowland soil usually contain 90 or 95 per cent. Some upland soils, on the other hand, which are derived from igneous or ancient sedimentary rocks, and have not been subjected to such drastic weathering, may retain much more of the parent rock in their sand and silt fractions. Because the sand particles are irregular, they trap air in the spaces between them. Of an

Opposite (top) Slime mould. This belongs to a group of very simple organisms, common in woodlands, with both fungal and animal characteristics.

Opposite (bottom) Puffball

Below Stinkhorn

average clod of earth, only about 40 to 70 per cent is solid matter, the remainder consisting of empty spaces containing only water and air. Silt particles cause waterlogging by blocking these pore spaces and thus impeding drainage.

Clay is composed of particles with a diameter of less than 0·002mm. It is sticky when wet, but shrinks as it dries to become hard, almost like brick. The clay minerals remain stable as long as the soil is neutral or only slightly acid or basic, as is normal in most of Great Britain; but they are greatly modified by the alkalinity of calcium carbonate and by acids from the decay of organic matter. Some of the calcium carbonate in the soil is formed during the weathering of the parent rocks, and some during the decomposition of plant materials. Most, however, is derived from chalk and limestone formations. The clay soils of the British Isles were originally covered with forest, and their clearance must have been a severe task for our Celtic and Saxon ancestors, who possessed only cumbersome implements and slow-moving oxen or horses – sometimes as many as four of which were needed to draw a single-share plough.

Clay-mineral particles, so small that they cannot be distinguished with a light microscope, even under high power, are often present as colloidal material. (A colloid is a glue or jelly-like substance. Unlike those of crystalloids, its particles may consist of large protein molecules. They do not readily diffuse through semi-permeable membranes.) Colloidal clay, together with colloidal humus, forms a complex whose particles are so intimately associated that it is difficult to separate them without materially affecting their chemical and physical properties. When calcium is present in sufficient quantity, it imparts physical and chemical stability to the clay–humus complex. By causing the fine colloidal particles to aggregate, it gives a granular or 'crumb' structure to very fine-grained clays, which, without calcium, are

Stag's horn

unfavourable to many forms of life. This information is vital if the setting up of a nature reserve is being considered. Soils can be 'improved', but only after they have been analysed. Soil crumbs increase the total pore space in the soil, allowing good aeration and drainage.

Humus production

The far-reaching importance of bacterial action in the chemical decomposition of organic matter has long been known; but numerous other microscopic organisms are also involved. The depth of the layer of organic litter on the surface of the soil is of prime importance in determining its quality. Decomposition and decay are rapid in alkaline soils. Here, bacteria and fungi break down cellulose, while bacteria also attack lignin (cellulose and lignin are the structural materials of which plants are composed; most animals are unable to digest them). When numerous larger animals, such as earthworms and insects, are present in alkaline soils, humus becomes completely mixed with the mineral components of the soil to form brown forest earths. In contrast, acid soils are unfavourable to bacteria and larger soil animals, while fungi have relatively little effect upon lignin. Organic acids are produced which tend to make the soil even more acid. The surface litter on acid soils is largely undecomposed, and the humus and mineral components of the soil are differentiated into well defined layers. One group of soils of this kind, the podsols, may be associated with various types of woodland in Britain. They consist of litter, with a leached layer beneath, which overlies a dark brown layer of deposition.

In addition to the two main climatic types of mature soil occurring in the British Isles – brown earths and podsols – various other soil types may be formed under local conditions. These include gley soils, which are seasonally or almost permanently waterlogged. As they are poorly aerated the micro-organisms they contain cause the chemical reduction of certain elements – particularly iron and manganese. Peat soils occur under conditions of permanent waterlogging and oxygen deficiency, while rendzinas are soils formed from limestone and chalk, on which the calcium carbonate has an overwhelming effect. They are permanently 'immature', being added to from below as the gradual solution of the calcium carbonate leaves behind insoluble mineral particles. Below the dense, dark surface of humus, a chalk soil is white or grey and passes down immediately into weathered limestone. In places where minerals accumulate over the limestone the surface layer may even become acidic.

Soils are not distinctly separable in the same way that plants and animals belong to distinct species, for one soil type usually grades into another. In addition to the three main groups of mature soil – brown forest earths, podsols and peat – the permanently immature rendzinas, and the gley soils described above, immature soils are not uncommon in Britain. They occur where human activity, glaciation, or river action has recently removed the original soil, exposing the underlying rocks. Some soils are immature because they exist on steep slopes, where the soil can never become mature. Only brown earths, podsols and rendzinas support woodland in the British Isles.

Leaching and stratification

In Britain, part of the rain falling on the

Above Sulphur polypore
Below Shaggy ink cap

surface of the soil is evaporated or, after penetrating a short distance, is taken up and transpired by plants. Part may run off the surface, while the remainder soaks through the soil and causes 'leaching'. As it percolates through the topsoil, water dissolves and removes the less insoluble components, depleting the upper horizons of iron, aluminium, calcium, magnesium, sodium and potassium. In consequence, the soil tends to become bleached, impoverished and acidic, while dark-coloured and/or ochreous layers are formed below, where humus and hydrated oxides of iron and aluminium respectively have been precipitated. Fine particles of clay

Left Morel

Below Ganoderma

are also moved downwards and, when deposited, form a layer containing more clay than the layers above and below it. Leaching is the process by which podsols are formed through the weathering of acidic rock in humid temperate climates.

The continual effect of weathering and leaching leads to the development of 'stratification' – the differentiation of distinct horizons from the soil surface down to the unaltered parent material formed from the underlying rocks. The various strata or horizons constitute the 'soil profile', a conspicuous feature of natural undisturbed soils which have reached a state of equilibrium with soil-forming agencies.

A soil profile (see Figure 4) consists of several horizons, each having characteristic physical and chemical properties. At the surface lies the litter or L layer – often called

by the Swedish term Förna (Fö) – which consists of undecomposed material. Beneath this lies the humus or A_0 layer, composed of amorphous organic matter which has lost its original structure. Then comes a varying number of layers of topsoil, A. The first of these, A_1, is a dark-coloured horizon containing a relatively high content of organic matter mixed with mineral fragments. It tends to be thin in forest soils. The A_2 (or E) horizon is frequently ashy grey and is the zone of maximum leaching. Sometimes, as in coniferous forest, the organic matter occurs in various stages of decomposition as separate layers (0 horizons) at the surface of the mineral soil. The underlying B horizons of subsoil tend to be darker in colour because

Blusher

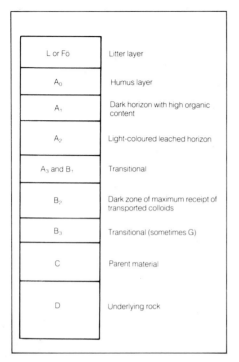

L or Fö	Litter layer
A₀	Humus layer
A₁	Dark horizon with high organic content
A₂	Light-coloured leached horizon
A₃ and B₁	Transitional
B₂	Dark zone of maximum receipt of transported colloids
B₃	Transitional (sometimes G)
C	Parent material
D	Underlying rock

Figure 4 Nomenclature of soil horizons.

they are enriched by iron and aluminium compounds, clay and humus. A lighter-coloured C horizon of parent material then grades into the D horizon of bedrock. This description is especially applicable to podsols (see Figure 5). In brown forest earths, the profile is more uniformly coloured throughout, with a darker, humus-rich A₁ horizon on top, grading into somewhat lighter-coloured subsoil. Brown earths are usually slightly acid, never alkaline, and are most typically developed on a clay or loam subsoil. In rendzinas or 'humus-carbonate' soils there is no appreciable B horizon. The upper horizon, usually dark brown, sometimes with a whitish tinge when on chalk, grades directly into lighter-coloured parent rock.

The humus typical of brown earths is usually derived from broad-leaved trees and is called 'mull'. In coniferous forests there is a more acid type of raw humus, known as 'mor', in which, as already mentioned, fungi, on or near the surface, are the chief agents of humus decay. Intermediate between mull and mor is 'moder', which has a richer and more varied fauna than mor, although plant remains are not broken down to the same extent as in mull. Moder tends to be considerably eaten into and mixed with faecal matter, yet is not matted together as raw humus, and some mineral matter is also incorporated. Mor and acid moder are the types of humus characteristic of podsols.

The relief of the ground strongly affects the movement and accumulation of water. Where the ground is flat and run-off is impeded, surface waterlogging may result in the formation of surface-water gley soils. If, on the other hand, the water percolates rapidly until it reaches the water table, it may leave well drained, high, flat land, in the form of podsol or brown earth (see Figure 6).

The study of woodland soils

In studying the weathering of rocks and the formation of soil, all available climatic and physical data should be noted. Although rainfall is undoubtedly the most important, other factors, such as temperature, play a part in soil formation. Temperature affects the speed of both chemical and biological changes, the balance between precipitation and evaporation determines the amount of leaching that takes place, and so on. In its turn, climate is considerably affected by altitude.

Soil profiles can be studied from specially dug pits or, more simply, by the use of a soil auger or soil sampler (Figure 7). The first of these is a steel instrument with a screw at the base. In use it is screwed 15cm (6 inches) into the ground and pulled out. After the first 15cm of soil have been examined and dis-

Figure 5 (opposite) Soil profiles: podsol, brown forest earth, and rendzina.

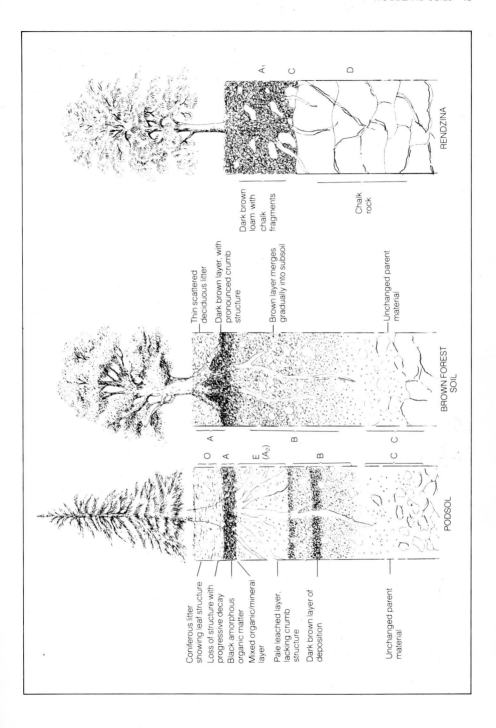

PODSOL

Coniferous litter
showing leaf structure

Loss of structure with
progressive decay

Black amorphous
organic matter

Mixed organic/mineral
layer

Pale leached layer,
lacking crumb
structure

Dark brown layer of
deposition

Unchanged parent
material

O
A
E (A₂)
B
C

BROWN FOREST
SOIL

Thin scattered
deciduous litter

Dark brown layer, with
pronounced crumb
structure

Brown layer merges
gradually into subsoil

Unchanged parent
material

A
B
C

RENDZINA

A₁
C
D

Dark brown
loam with
chalk
fragments

Chalk
rock

Right Dryad's saddle

Opposite Orange peel

Below Boletus

carded, it is put into the same hole and screwed in to a depth of 30cm. The process is again repeated to a depth of 90cm. A soil sampler consists of a cylindrical corer which is forced into the ground. When filled with earth, it is removed and the sample examined directly or placed in a bag for subsequent study in the laboratory. The process is then repeated and the hole gradually deepened.

Differences of aspect, and thus of insolation, sometimes affect vegetation markedly. Southern slopes tend to be open grassland while north-facing slopes are moister and more characteristic of woodland. Slopes can be measured by means of a clinometer. A simple, home-made instrument can be constructed consisting of a protractor whose base is aligned with the ground while a weighted string indicates the angle from the vertical.

The colour of the soil can be compared with a series of standard colours; the acidity or alkalinity measured with the aid of a soil-testing indicator. This consists of a neutral liquid which changes colour according to the reaction of the soil with which it has been placed in contact. The colour is matched to a chart. Calcium carbonate content can be assessed by the amount of effervescence produced with dilute hydrochloric acid.

Recognition of soil types is based on the relative proportions of mineral grain sizes as these affect textural properties. Moist soil is moulded in the hand and small amounts passed through the thumb and index finger and the type assessed, without the use of apparatus, as described by John Sankey in his *Guide to Field Biology*. Light, sandy soils are rough or gritty, and cohere weakly. Their capacity to retain water or plant nutrients is small. Heavy clay soils are sticky when wet and both coherent and pliable when moist.

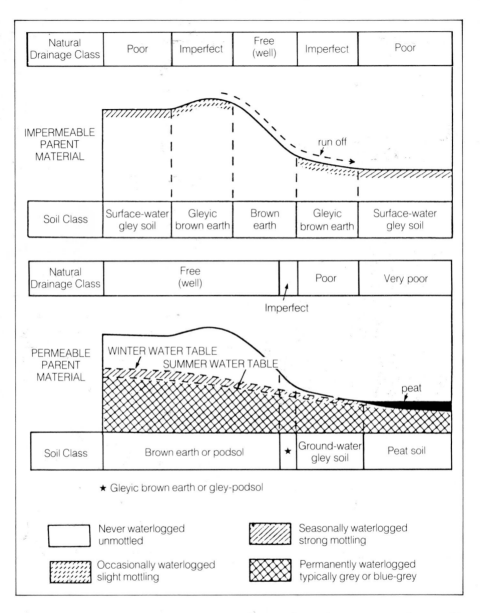

Figure 6 Effect of relief and hydrology on soil and drainage.

Silty soils are coherent without being sticky, while loamy soils contain a mixture of all three grades. Soil structure may be 'crumb' or 'fine blocky' with small aggregates of particles, 'coarse blocky' when these are equidimensional, or 'prismatic' when they are elongated. Other properties to be noted

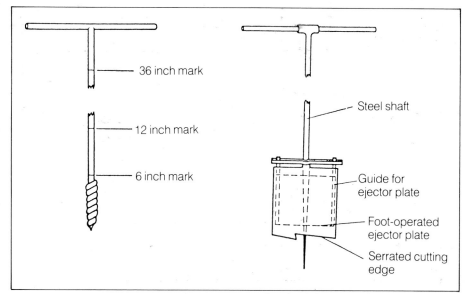

Figure 7 Soil auger and soil sampler.

include the depth of root penetration and the activities of soil animals, such as earthworms, which can be observed directly.

The environment of a plant can be analysed under various headings: climatic, edaphic (soil) and biotic factors. Many small plants are restricted to certain microhabitats each with its own microclimate. Light, temperature, moisture and so on within a wood are often quite different from those in open country where the same general climate prevails. Techniques for the study of the microclimates of both plants and animals are outlined at the end of this chapter.

Soil organisms

The organisms which inhabit the soil, and which are responsible for creating humus by decomposing organic litter and carrying it down into the earth, vary in size from viruses – so small that they become visible only under an electron microscope – to earthworms and the moles that feed on them, and even rabbits and badgers. As a matter of convenience, they can be divided into three groups: micro-organisms too small to be seen without the aid of a microscope; invertebrates, including worms, mites, springtails, millipedes and insects; and burrowing vertebrate animals, which will be discussed in Chapter 4.

Micro-organisms

The micro-organisms of British woodland soils include viruses and bacteria, actinomycetes, fungi, unicellular algae and Protozoa. Viruses are parasitic and can multiply only within living cells. Some plant viruses, however, may remain infective and quiescent in the soil for several months. Others are transmitted from one plant to another by fungi, nematodes and other soil organisms. Bacteriophages may be more complex than viruses. They are parasites of bacteria and actinomycetes. When a bacterial cell becomes infected, the phage particles multiply within it until the host cell ruptures, releasing large numbers of new bacteriophages. The extent to which phages limit the numbers of soil bacteria is not known but bacteria seldom occur without bacteriophages also being

Above Shaggy pholiota   **Below** Fungus on rotting wood

present. Some are extremely host-specific, others are able to infect several different species of bacteria.

Bacteria Of all soil organisms, bacteria are the most numerous. They play essential roles in the formation of humus, in fixing nitrogen and in many other soil processes. More than 10^9 bacterial cells may occur within a gram of rich forest soil, which is equivalent to a live weight of 1,360kg per hectare (3,000lb per acre). The most common kinds are rod-shaped – usually less than one micron in width and three or four microns long (a micron is one thousandth of a millimetre). Many swim about actively in the film of water that coats the soil particles by means of whip-like flagella. These are borne in tufts at the end, or distributed around the edge of the cell. Bacteria are believed to improve the crumb structure of the soil by cementing together mineral particles and humus.

Many bacteria multiply rapidly when conditions are favourable, but most soil-inhabiting species do not do so for long, because the nutrients are soon exhausted. Nevertheless, they have the potentiality to take immediate advantage of any new food source. When conditions are unfavourable, on the other hand, thick-walled resistant spores are often formed. Most soil bacteria are aerobic and cannot grow unless oxygen is present – although some are able to tolerate anaerobic conditions characteristic of water-logged soils. Anaerobic conditions may also develop locally, even in well drained soils, when all the oxygen has been used up by aerobic bacteria. Soil bacteria are able to satisfy their nutritional requirements in many different ways. Some require organic compounds, as do fungi and animals; others are able to synthesise organic compounds from atmospheric carbon dioxide, obtaining energy either from sunlight or by oxidising inorganic substances. The former are more numerous. Some soil bacteria require complex nitrogenous compounds, but most can make use of ammonium salts or nitrates. Several species are able to fix atmospheric nitrogen and thereby enrich the soil in the absence of any other fertiliser.

Actinomycetes and fungi Actinomycetes are organisms in many ways intermediate between bacteria and fungi. Their fine, branching networks of filaments, less than one micron in diameter and with few cross walls, are common in brown forest earths and rendzina soils, but actinomycetes cannot tolerate acid conditions and are not found in podsols. Reproduction takes place by fragmentation of the filaments or, more often, by the formation of spores. Many soil-inhabiting actinomycetes produce antibiotics which inhibit the bacteria and fungi that might otherwise compete with them. *Streptomyces griseus* is a well known example since it produces the medicinally important streptomycin.

Fungi are probably almost as important as bacteria in contributing to soil processes or plant nutrition in neutral and alkaline soils. They are even more important in podsols, since they usually tolerate acid conditions better than bacteria do.

Soil fungi vary from primitive unicellular species to the toadstools with their large and complex fruiting bodies. The volume of fungal threads or 'hyphae' in woodland soil is comparable with that of bacteria – about 2,000 million cubic microns per gram, or about 0·2 per cent of the soil volume. Many of them produce spores and some form symbiotic associations or 'mycorrhiza' with the roots of trees. For example, the fly agaric and boletus fungi form mycorrhiza with birch trees. Moulds of the genus *Penicillium*, which produce valuable antibiotic substances, are also common soil fungi.

Most soil fungi assist in decomposing organic matter in the soil. Fungi are also primarily responsible for the breakdown of woody tissues, since a major constituent of wood and all secondarily thickened plant tissues is lignin. This is readily attacked by fungal hyphae but not by bacteria. Many fungi also decompose cellulose and may attack this substance even before bacteria do. Others are parasitic on plants, especially seedlings, and soil animals such as nematode worms. Their hyphae form nooses that contract and strangle the nematodes, or have sticky pads that adhere to them (Figure 10).

Algae Because they are green and require sunlight for photosynthesis, soil algae are invariably found on or near the surface of the soil. Only a few species, which have lost their chlorophyll, are able to live in the dark, where they are dependent upon organic compounds synthesised by green plants.

Protozoa The rich flora of bacteria in woodland soil provides nourishment for many protozoan species, including amoebae, flagellates and ciliates – of which the flagellates are most numerous and the ciliates comparatively scarce. Most soil Protozoa encyst (enter a state of suspended animation beneath a protective covering) when conditions are unfavourable. Cysts are more resistant to heat and drought than the active phases, and are easily dispersed over considerable distances by the wind. They may remain viable for several decades and recover when moistened.

Invertebrates

Some animals of woodland soils, such as nematodes, earthworms and moles, spend their entire lives in the soil; while others, including burrowing insects, newts, reptiles and rodents, spend only part of their time – or specific stages of their life cycles – underground, and are therefore only temporary soil fauna. Such creatures can also be classified according to whether they actually burrow or inhabit existing spaces in the earth. Many of the protozoans are confined to the water film surrounding the soil particles. Earthworms,

slugs and some insect larvae likewise require moist conditions and so are intermediate between the aquatic and the aerial fauna. Another criterion for the classification of soil animals is according to their feeding habits. Some 'phytophagous' forms feed on living plant material. These include slugs, snails, symphylids and many insects – both larvae and adults. 'Saprophagous' animals feed on dead materials, both plant and animal. Earthworms, millipedes, insect larvae, ants and other insects do so extensively – they are consequently important for the formation of humus and its incorporation into the soil. 'Carnivorous' animals include centipedes, false-scorpions, ground spiders, carabid and staphylinid beetles and their larvae, lizards, snakes, moles, and so on. The numbers of soil-dwelling animals are extremely large. Their roles in the flow of energy, nitrogen cycle and food chains in British woodlands will be discussed in the final chapter of this book.

The litter and humus layers of woodland soil are especially rich in woodlice, myriapods, arachnids and insects, which will be discussed in the next chapter. They provide a happy hunting ground for many a keen naturalist. The soil, litter, fallen logs, cracks in tree trunks and spaces under bark, as well as rodent burrows, mossy banks and lichen-covered rocks, provide innumerable micro-habitats, each with its own characteristic fauna which well repays investigation.

Methods of investigating soil animals

The study of 'cryptozoic' animals – that is, animals which lead hidden lives – in their micro-environments is rather more complicated than the direct observations of animals that live above ground and in the open. The best way to investigate the behaviour of animals beneath the soil surface is to enclose soil and humus in boxes with glass sides. These are covered to exclude the light, except when observations are being made. Animals, plant roots and fungi can be watched through the glass, either with the naked eye or with a low-power microscope. Slow-growing objects, such as fungal hyphae and plant roots, can be sketched and photographed at regular intervals. The activities of earthworms can be studied simply by placing the animals in cages made from two pieces of glass slotted into a frame so that they are 1–2cm apart. The worms are able to burrow when the cage is filled with soil but the pieces of glass are so close together that the burrows can be seen through them. Again, the glass plates need to be covered so that the worms are in darkness except when they are being

Above Brittle caps

Below Spotted tough shank

Above Jew's ear

Below Parasol mushrooms

Buff meadow cap

observed. To see how different species mix the soil, the cages should be filled with alternating layers of soil of different colours or textures. The production of worm casts and the burial of leaf litter can also be studied in the field.

Population studies

In order to obtain estimates of the numbers of animals present in leaf litter and soil, the material to be sampled (perhaps extracted by a soil sampler) is placed in a small sieve resting above a glass funnel. Heat from an electric light bulb, suspended in a metal cylinder over the sieve, dries out the soil and litter, so that its inhabitants move downwards and fall into the funnel. This directs them into a collecting vessel containing alcohol or some other fixative. Not all kinds of organism are extracted with equal efficiency, and most workers design their own modification of this basic principle. Various flotation methods have also been devised to extract immobile resting stages such as eggs, cocoons and pupae. The sample is broken up into a suitable container, frozen for several days and then thawed to fragment the soil crumbs. It is next washed through a sieve to eliminate stones and vegetable matter. Finally, xylene (or

paraffin) is shaken up with the water. Micro-arthropods that come in contact with the xylene collect on the xylene-water interface formed when the xylene separates into a layer floating on the water. Other organic material remains in the water beneath the xylene layer.

Pitfall traps, consisting of jars or tins sunk flush with the soil surface, provide a convenient means of collecting animals that are active on the surface of the ground – particularly woodlice, millipedes, centipedes, spiders, harvest spiders and beetles. The traps contain a preservative, and may be provided with a cover to exclude rainwater and to prevent shrews and mice falling in. If a fixative, such as a 5% solution of ethylene glycol, is not present, the predatory forms may well eat all the other inmates before the trap can be emptied.

An estimate of the total population of a species in a particular area can sometimes be made by the 'marking and recapture' method. Individuals are caught, marked with cellulose paint, and released. After they have been allowed time to redistribute themselves in the population, a second catch is made. The number of marked individuals in the second catch is then compared with the number of unmarked individuals. From this ratio, the total population can be calculated as follows:

$$\frac{\text{Total number first} \atop \text{caught and marked} \times \text{Total number collected} \atop \text{in second sample}}{\text{Number of marked individuals} \atop \text{in the second sample}}$$

However, the method depends on certain assumptions for the estimate obtained to be valid. The catches have to be random samples of the total population, while marked and unmarked individuals must be caught with equal ease. It is often difficult, in practice, to ensure that these assumptions are satisfied. In the case of pitfall traps, for example, it is difficult to decide how far from their place of capture to release the marked individuals, or to be sure that they become properly redistributed in the population which the traps are sampling before the second catch is made. Again, some kinds of soil animals, such as earthworms and slugs, cannot be marked satisfactorily.

Microclimatic measurements

Two factors have to be taken into consideration in the design of apparatus for the measurement of physical conditions within confined spaces. First, the sensory elements of the instruments to be used must be sufficiently small and, second, it should be possible to take readings some distance away from them. Although a mercury thermometer can be used for measuring temperatures beneath the surface of the soil, or in soft, rotting wood, its large size is a disadvantage because there may be a temperature gradient in the soil or wood. Then there is a tendency for heat to be conducted from the bulb along the stem so that the thermometer itself affects the microclimate it is supposed to be measuring. Finally, the proximity of the sensing and reading parts of the instrument limits its use, and it cannot be used to measure air temperatures accurately when exposed to a source of radiant heat. Fortunately, reasonably inexpensive electronic apparatus is available, which is suitable for measuring both temperature and relative humidity in small spaces.

Relative humidity can also be measured by exposing in the microhabitat small pieces of paper soaked in a solution of cobalt thiocyanate. Cobalt thiocyanate paper is prepared commercially and is readily available. It changes colour from red to blue when the humidity decreases. Papers are exposed in an environment in which humidity is to be determined, and are then mounted in liquid paraffin between a piece of colourless glass and a small white tile, as soon as they have reached equilibrium. They are later matched in a comparator with standards made of coloured glass. Alternatively, the experimenter can make his own standards with painted paper which has been matched with cobalt thiocyanate papers exposed to known humidities. The only problem is to obtain the known humidities in which to expose cobalt thiocyanate paper standards in the first instance. Controlled humidities can easily be prepared, however, from selections of sulphuric acid, potassium hydroxide and other salts. Details of the method are given in my book *Microecology*, which is listed in the Bibliography.

Soil moisture can be estimated by drying a known weight of earth at 100°C until no further loss in weight occurs, and then reweighing to determine the amount of water that has been lost in evaporation. More complicated and time-consuming techniques have also been employed, which involve measurement of the suction pressure of the water in soil samples. Light intensity can only be measured satisfactorily by means of a photographic exposure meter or a photoelectric cell; wind speed by a small anemometer; and alkalinity or acidity (hydrogen ion concentration), as already described, with the aid of indicator solutions.

Although many of the techniques mentioned above are somewhat imprecise, this does not really matter since they can be used for *comparing* one microclimate with another. Such comparisons, in relation to the faunas of the microhabitats being investigated, are what interests the naturalist. For example, even though a cup-type anemometer cannot measure wind speed right against the trunk of a tree, it will give some indication of differences in wind speed between one night and another. Simple counts on different nights in a selected habitat will immediately indicate an inverse relationship between wind speed and the number of woodlice, centipedes and millipedes abroad. It is more interesting to establish such a relationship than to worry about the exact wind speeds or evaporation rates that are actually being experienced by the animals.

4 Invertebrates

The organisms that inhabit soil, leaf litter, rotting logs, holes in trees, the spaces beneath bark and such habitats can be conveniently divided into two major categories according to their sizes. Micro-organisms, which can be studied only with the aid of a microscope and culture plates (discussed in the last chapter), and macro-organisms, which are visible with the naked eye. With a few notable exceptions, naturalists tend to be concerned mainly with larger, multicellular organisms. These can be grouped in various different ways. One type of classification depends upon feeding habits – phytophagous, saprophagous or carnivorous. Another method is to classify according to taxonomic position in the animal kingdom – nematodes, earthworms, molluscs, arthropods and vertebrates. This is the approach used in this book.

This chapter is concerned with soil animals, animals that lead hidden lives – the 'cryptozoa' – and animals that live on tree trunks and foliage, including flying insects, web-building spiders, and so on.

Soil animals and cryptozoans

The animals described here range in size from microscopic eelworms, which cannot be discerned with the naked eye, to earthworms, larval stag beetles, and other larger insects. Some idea of the approximate sizes and numbers of invertebrate animals found in a cubic decimetre of woodland soil is given in the following table:

	Sizes	Numbers
Protozoa	0·01–0·3mm	1,500,000,000
Nematodes	0·3–1·0mm	50,000
Small arthropods	1·0–5·0mm	350
Large arthropods	10–30mm	25
Earthworms	50–200mm	2

Some species are found exclusively in soil; others are also to be found in the layer of leaf litter resting on it, on the trunks of trees, and in the field layer of vegetation. Most of them are inconspicuous and lead secretive lives. As Theodore Savory wrote in 1971, 'The animals we see around us – the cows and horses, dogs and cats, eagles and crocodiles, sharks and hippopotamuses – represent the familiar few; the teeming multitudes are to be found hidden in the earth, or beneath the debris that covers much of the earth's surface.'

The name 'cryptozoa' was coined by Arthur Dendy in 1895 to include 'the assemblage of small terrestrial animals found dwelling in darkness beneath stones, rotten

Right Brown hairstreak

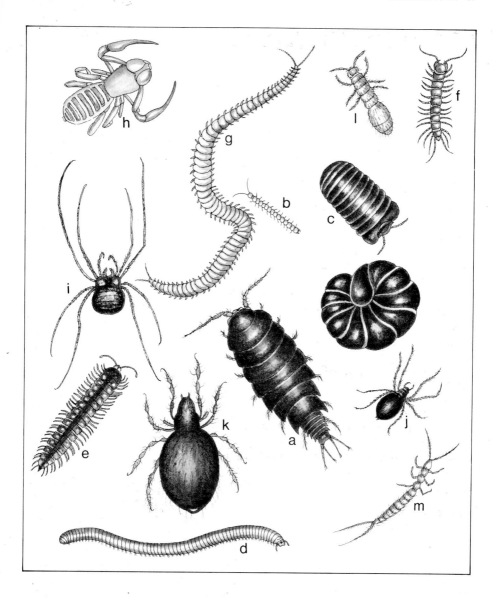

Figure 8 Some typical cryptozoic animals: (a) woodlouse (Isopoda: Trichoniscidae); (b) symphylid (Symphyla: Scutigerellidae); (c) pill millipede (Diplopoda: Glomeridae); (d) false-wireworm (Diplopoda: Iulidae); (e) flat-backed millipede (Diplopoda: Polydesmidae); (f) lithobiid centipede (Chilopoda: Lithobiidae); (g) geophilid centipede (Chilopoda: Geophilidae); (h) false-scorpion (Pseudoscorpiones: Chthoniidae); (i) harvest-spider (Opiliones: Nemastomatidae); (j) spider (Araneae: Linyphiidae); (k) beetle mite (Acari: Oribatei); (l) springtail (Collembola: Poduridae); (m) bristletail (Diplura: Campodeidae). (Drawings not to scale.)

logs, the bark of trees and in other similar situations'. Some of them are illustrated in Figure 8. The cryptozoa are usually distinct from soil animals although, as in other ecological groupings, there are many overlaps. The cryptosphere, in which cryptozoic animals dwell, consists of fallen leaves that lie decaying on the earth's surface, rotting logs, the spaces underneath bark, cracks in tree trunks, the undersurfaces of rocks and stones, slates, pottery and other refuse.

Size

Soil-dwelling and cryptozoic animals are generally small, and their ways of life are governed principally by the physical consequences that follow from this. Size influences the vitally important relationship between volume and surface area. Other things being equal, the ratio of surface area to volume increases with diminishing size. The smaller an animal is, the greater its surface area with respect to volume.

The relatively enormous surface area of small animals in relation to their volume poses problems of water conservation. Their physiology and behaviour are, consequently, very largely concerned with the perpetual struggle to avoid drying up. The integuments or cuticles of most insects and arachnids are coated with an extremely thin layer of waterproof wax. This prevents them from losing their precious water too rapidly by evaporation into the atmosphere. But for this, day-flying moths and butterflies, hoverflies and bumble-bees would not be able to be active in sunlight – because they would dry up so fast. Wolf spiders could not run across the dry surface of the ground, nor could web-building species remain in the open.

Not all small animals have solved the problem of their large surface to volume ratio in the same way. Earthworms, centipedes, millipedes and woodlice, for example, do not possess waterproof coverings. Instead, they have to remain in damp environments most of the time, seldom emerging from their retreats except at night when the temperature falls and the relative humidity of the atmosphere increases. The pill woodlouse (illustrated in Figure 9) is more resistant to evaporation than other kinds of woodlouse, and this is the species that is occasionally to be seen wandering around in dry places during the daytime. The animals discussed in this chapter (apart from some insects and arachnids) tend, in general, to avoid drought and light, and to exhibit nocturnal patterns of behaviour. Among those most dependent upon high humidity are delicate, unpigmented arthropods such as pauropods, symphylids, bristletails, and springtails. The least drought-resistant types, which are usually also the smallest, occur deeper down in narrower crevices of the soil and litter where the evaporating power of the air ('saturation deficiency') is lowest. Seasonal as well as daily vertical migrations depend mainly on the water content of the soil, the animals descending in summer when the surface layers dry out. (How deep an animal goes also depends on how much air there is in the burrow.) Animals that feed on plant material are least affected, because they can compensate for water loss by feeding on succulent roots. They also save energy through not having to chase prey, though their food is less nutritious.

The success of soil and cryptozoic animals, demonstrated by their wide distribution and diversity, is proof that small size confers advantages as well as disadvantages. In a world of predation and sudden death a small animal can hide easily and has a greater range of refuges available to it. Small animals usually reach maturity relatively quickly, so that rapid increases in number are possible. Food is readily available for small creatures, and may be consumed without delay. Larger animals must spend relatively more time and energy in finding their food, and take longer eating it. On the other hand, small animals not only dry

Above Snake fly, an uncommon insect of oaks and pines.

Left Aggregating sphecid wasps.

Below Angle shades moth

Figure 9 Common British woodlice: (a) *Trichoniscus*; (b) *Philoscia*; (c) *Oniscus*; (d) *Porcellio*; (e) *Armadillidium* (pill woodlouse).

up more quickly than larger ones, but they are more easily trapped and drowned by a film of water. Tactile senses are more important to them than vision, the ability to burrow and push their way into crevices more important than speed. Survival represents the achievement of a satisfactory compromise between the opposing advantages and disadvantages of small size in the particular environments inhabited by soil-dwelling and cryptozoic animals.

Nematodes

After the Protozoa, nematode worms are the most abundant of woodland animals. Some are shown in Figure 10. As many as 10,000

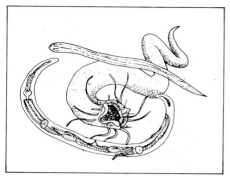

Figure 10 (above)   Soil nematodes – the central one is a predator (body lengths around 1mm).

Right Greater stag-beetle, with larvae, and lesser stag-beetle.

individuals per millilitre may be found in suitable woodland soils. Nematodes are also extremely numerous parasites of plants and animals. It is said that if all living organisms other than nematodes were to disappear their outlines would still remain as ghostly images – composed of the countless tiny nematode parasites that inhabit their tissues. Free-living, soil-inhabiting species belong to the nematode group known as 'eelworms'. These secrete slime, which works like a film of oil, cutting down friction and making movement easier. They move in the soil through cracks, squeezing themselves into tiny spaces. Eel-worms are most numerous in the top layer of the soil, especially where it is penetrated by the roots of plants. Some feed on detritus and decomposing animal or vegetable matter, others on bacteria and soil algae. Many are

partly parasitic on the roots of plants, but relatively few are positively harmful to their hosts. Those that are may be crop pests, but do not damage woodland plants.

Predatory nematodes feed on protozoans, water bears, rotifers and other nematodes. Stag beetles, whose larvae develop in very rotten wood, and which remain there in the adult state for long periods, are usually heavily infested with nematode worms. The larvae of one species of nematode regularly penetrate the bodies of earthworms. Here they remain until the worm dies, when they develop further and cause rapid decomposition of the corpse.

The enemies of nematodes include a variety of predatory arthropods, including beetle

Figure 11   Nematode snared by a fungus.

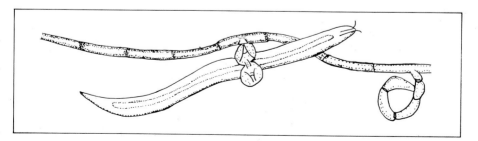

mites of several species. Certain fungi trap nematodes with adhesive discs or by rings attached to their hyphae. These rings are contractile, collar-like outgrowths which constrict the bodies of the nematode worms unfortunate enough to enter them, as shown in Figure 11. The fungus then dissolves the cuticle, drives a tube into the body of the nematode, and absorbs its internal organs. Some soil fungi may have non-constricting ring traps which act passively, while the pointed spores of others bore into nematode cuticles and form mycelia within the animals' bodies.

The general significance of nematode worms for the metabolism of the soil lies in the fact that they are continually decomposing plant material, especially roots, without actually damaging the plants to a noticeable degree. At the same time, they can multiply extremely rapidly in the presence of decaying plant and animal materials, and thereby enrich the soil with organic matter.

One of the most satisfactory methods for collecting nematodes from soil or plant material is to use a funnel with a piece of rubber tubing attached to the stem which can be closed with a spring clip. The funnel, held in a clamp, is almost filled with water. Soil containing the nematodes to be extracted is crumbled onto a paper tissue, resting on a piece of wire gauze. This is placed in the funnel so that the soil sample is immersed in water. Nematodes leave the soil, pass through the paper and, being heavier than water, sink to the bottom of the funnel stem from which, after some hours, they can be withdrawn by releasing the spring clip. Plant material should be cut into small pieces or minced before the nematodes are extracted in this way. Soil-dwelling nematodes are so small that they must be studied with the aid of a high power microscope.

Figure 12 (right) A soil rotifer (body length 0.5mm).

Rotifers and water bears

These two groups include typical microscopic inhabitants of fresh water, but are not taxonomically related. Some species of each are, however, found in damp woodland soil and moss. Certain rotifers (Figure 12), like Protozoa (p. 52), form cysts when conditions are unfavourable. In this state, they are very resistant to desiccation and to high and low temperatures. The food of rotifers consists of plant and animal remains, as well as Protozoa. Tardigrades, or water bears (Figure 13), are also regular inhabitants of moss cushions, from which, like rotifers, they can be extracted when the moss is mixed with pieces of ice and placed in a glass funnel. Water bears are easily recognised by their four pairs of stumpy, claw-bearing legs and their conical snouts. Their food consists of organic detritus, moss, protozoans, nematodes and rotifers. Like rotifers, tardigrades can withstand heat, cold and drought when encysted.

Earthworms

The population of earthworms in woodland soils varies from about 60 to 260 per m^2. This is equivalent to some 150–660 tonnes per km^2. Soils that are poor in organic matter do not usually support large numbers of earthworms. Conversely, if there are few worms,

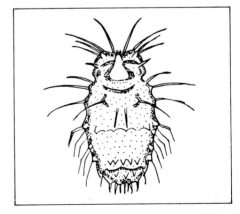

Figure 13 A water bear (body length 0.2mm).

decaying organic matter usually lies in a thick mat on the soil surface, both in woodlands and grasslands. The presence of decaying leaves, however, usually favours the multiplication of earthworms, which have been shown to consume more oak and beech litter than all other soil invertebrates put together. The smaller species that feed on litter in woodlands (shown in Figure 14) produce casts which consist almost entirely of fragmented litter, whereas larger species consume a high proportion of soil and there is less organic matter in their casts.

Earthworms have moist skins and lose water rapidly in dry air. Water constitutes between 70 and 90 per cent of their body weight, and the prevention of water loss is a major problem for them in dry weather. As the soil dries, they burrow downwards. During prolonged drought, they hollow out small spaces in the ground which are lined with slime. This helps to prevent dehydration as the surrounding soil dries up. The worms do not feed at this time but roll themselves into tight balls, often forming one or two knots during the process. Their head and tail ends are tucked into the balls, reducing to a minimum the area from which evaporation can take place; and at the same time they may lose nearly two-thirds of their total body water without ill effects.

Field experiments on earthworms usually require only simple techniques. The most reliable way of assessing the number of as

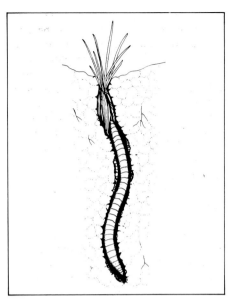

Figure 14 Earthworm dragging pine needles into its burrow.

many species as possible is to combine hand-sorting of soil samples of known volume with chemical extraction. The application of 25ml of 40 per cent formalin in 4·5 litres of water applied to 0·5m^2 of soil surface is very effective in bringing worms to the surface. The main disadvantage of this method is that not all species are recovered equally efficiently. Species with wide burrows come to the surface more readily than non-burrowing species. Both the temperature and the moisture of the soil affect the numbers of worms coming to the surface. The production of worm casts on the soil surface provides a useful measure of the activity of earthworms, while the feeding activity of larger species can be estimated from the amount of plant material gathered at the entrances to their burrows. Wooden frames are placed on areas of ground cleared of leaves. A known weight of dry fallen leaves is placed in the frame and the top covered with wire mesh to prevent them from blowing away or being disturbed

Oak eggar moth larvae

Green tiger beetle

by birds. After one or two months, the remaining leaves are removed, washed free of soil, dried and re-weighed. At the end of the experimental period the number of worms beneath the frames is estimated by hand sorting, applying formalin solution, or counting the burrow openings. The weight of leaves consumed by one worm and the total per square metre can then be calculated. The results obtained over different periods should be correlated with rainfall and temperature. Observation cages for studying worm behaviour are described in Chapter 3.

Snails and slugs

Terrestrial molluscs all belong to the same group, the pulmonates – so named because they breathe by means of lungs. Several species are found in British woodlands, some inhabiting the soil, others the litter layer; some feeding on the vegetation of the herb layer – which is rasped with the toothed 'radula' or tongue – others climbing the bark of trees at night. Not all slugs and snails are vegetarians, however. Some woodland snails feed on rotting wood, others prefer dead leaves. Many are extremely small. Slugs, too, enjoy a variety of diets, ranging from the fruiting bodies of fungi, algae, lichens, moss and other plant material. Some are predatory, eating earthworms. The pharynx of the slug is protruded. It is equipped with a sharp-toothed radula with which the end of the worm is seized; and the prey is swallowed by

Left Wingless female mottled umber moth.

retraction of the slug's pharynx. Often only a piece of the earthworm is torn off, and the process repeated. Some snails are predatory also, feeding upon worms and other snails. Many slugs and snails hibernate in winter, but some remain lively and continue to feed even when they are buried beneath a thick cover of snow. Most surface-dwelling snails withdraw into the litter and upper layers of the soil in late autumn. Here they hibernate and do not feed again until the following spring. The large Roman snail buries itself relatively deep in the soil and closes its shell with a chalky disc, the secretion of which is induced by cold weather.

Although snails and slugs are common members of the woodland fauna, many aspects of their ecology are little known and would repay further study. Snail populations can be estimated by the marking and recapture method (p. 54), but this is not applicable to slugs, which, lacking shells, cannot be marked with paint. In any case, it is not possible to separate the two parameters of activity and abundance. Results obtained by counting those seen on, say, a fifteen-minute walk after dark represent a combination of the effects of both activity and abundance. The method can, however, be used to relate different species to their habits, to study activity in relation to weather, and the seasonal occurrence of particular species or stages of development. Terrestrial molluscs can be reared easily in captivity to study their reproduction, the incubation period of the eggs, growth rates and longevity. The amount of food eaten can also be measured using a similar technique to that employed with earthworms. The extent to which organic matter is incorporated by molluscs into the mineral structure of the soil is, as yet, unknown.

Left Woodland snail

Woodlice

Most crustaceans are aquatic, inhabiting both sea and fresh water; but a few groups have succeeded in establishing themselves on land. Of these, only woodlice (Figure 9) are found in Britain, where they form an important element of the cryptozoa, especially on alkaline soils. One of the reasons why woodlice are successful land animals, even though, as already mentioned, their integument does not possess a waterproofing layer of wax, is that the young hatch and develop in a brood pouch. This characteristic probably developed in their marine ancestors as a defence against predatory enemies but, on land, it also has the advantage of protecting the young from drying up, which is the

Left Scarlet tiger

Below Gatekeeper

greatest threat to the existence of terrestrial arthropods. Indeed, as we have already seen, woodlice spend nearly all their lives in damp, dark hiding places from which they emerge only at night. Woodlice stay out longer on wet nights when the air has less drying power. Conversely, they are less active on windy nights because the wind removes the protective 'shell' of moist air around the transpiring animals. Naturalists can confirm the facts upon which this hypothesis is based by counting the number of woodlice wandering abroad on different nights, in the same area or on the same tree trunks, and correlating the results obtained with wind speed measured with a wind gauge or anemometer. If temperature and relative humidity are also measured, it will be found that the nocturnal emergence of woodlice and of other Arthropoda, as well as of molluscs, is related both to wind speed and to the temperature drop or corresponding rise in relative humidity that occur at dusk.

Woodlice, along with earthworms and millipedes, are often regarded as primary decomposers, the first link in the chain of organisms which breaks down dead plant material and mixes it with mineral particles to form soil. To the extent that they also eat their own faeces, however, they have to be

Above Dor beetle

Below Longhorn wasp-beetle

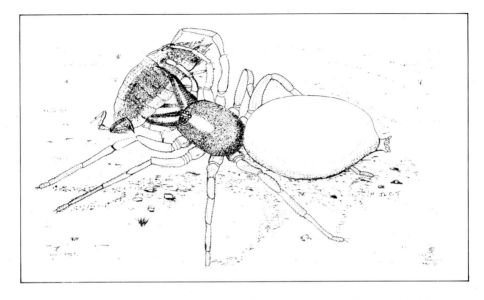

Figure 15 *Dysdera* spider eating a woodlouse.

regarded as secondary decomposers. More-over, it seems that vegetable matter has, to some degree, to be broken down by micro-organisms before woodlice will eat it. It may be significant that leaves containing a high concentration of tannins – which inhibit microbial activity – are disregarded until these substances have been leached out by rain. In contrast, ash and sycamore leaves, which have a low tannin content, are acceptable much sooner after they have fallen. A thick carpet of leaf litter gives the impression of abundant food for woodlice, an impression that may well be misleading since much of this litter is unpalatable until it has lain on the ground for some time. The varying palatability to woodlice of the various types of woodland leaf litter has not yet been properly investigated, although it is a research topic that might well be tackled by a keen naturalist. Another relates to the distribution and number of woodlice on soils of varying acidity and alkalinity.

Although a great variety of animals are known to eat woodlice under laboratory conditions, few records have been made of predation on them in the field. In captivity, woodlice are eaten by centipedes, spiders, harvest spiders, predatory beetles, frogs and toads, slow worms, little owls, shrews and hedgehogs. The intensity of predation in nature is uncertain, so any field observations are well worth recording. Analysis of the gut contents of potential predators gives rather uncertain results in most cases. This is because the integuments of woodlice tend to be broken up into tiny pieces when the animals are eaten, making the estimation of numbers present impossible. The use of radioisotope tracers, which can subsequently be detected in their predators, to label individual woodlice, involves the use of techniques that lie beyond the resources of most amateur naturalists. So, too, does the detection of woodlouse proteins in the guts of predators, using specific anti-bodies.

One genus of spider, of which there are two British species, is equipped with formidable jaws especially adapted for seizing woodlice in a pincer-like grip. *Dysdera*, to give the spider's

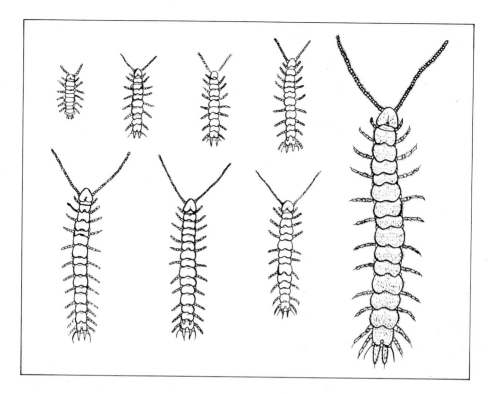

Figure 16 Stages in the development of a symphylid.

name, injects poison of such strength that the victim usually dies within a few seconds (Figure 15). Woodlice possess tegumental glands – one pair to each segment of the body – which secrete a fluid that repels most spiders. The large orange-coloured *Dysdera*, with its yellow abdomen, however, is completely undeterred by this defensive secretion.

Figure 17 A pauropod (body length 1.5mm).

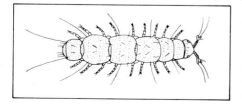

Woodlice can easily be marked with oil paint, and thus provide excellent material for population studies based on the capture and recapture technique described in the previous chapter. Although there is a growing body of knowledge concerning the population biology of woodlice, the processes by which their numbers are regulated in nature are little understood. Drought has been shown to affect some species very severely: growth and breeding cease, and the animals survive by vertical migration deep into the soil. Woodlice also tend to migrate downwards in winter from the soil–litter interface where they normally occur.

As subjects for behavioural experiments, woodlice have few equals. Many school and university student projects are concerned with unravelling the responses of woodlice to various environmental factors, for further

Above An ant-mimicking predatory clerid beetle. Many harmless arthropods gain protection from their ant-like appearance.

Left False-scorpion

information about which the woodland naturalist should see S. L. Sutton's thought-provoking book, *Woodlice*.

Myriapods

Pauropods and symphyla

Of the four orders of myriapods, pauropods and symphylans are extremely small in comparison with the better known centipedes and millipedes. Pauropods seldom exceed a millimetre in length, and move rather slowly. Their bodies consist of only a small number of segments, as shown in Figure 17. Pauropods may be broad or elongated, but can always be recognised by the branched antennae. Pauropods are most often seen beneath the bark of decaying tree stumps and in leaf litter, but they also occur in the soil. They are believed to feed on decomposing plant materials and fungi but, on account of their small size, have been little studied.

Symphylids look very much like small, white centipedes, seldom more than 1cm long. Their dorsal surfaces are protected by 15 plates, and they have 11 or 12 pairs of legs, though young animals have fewer seg-

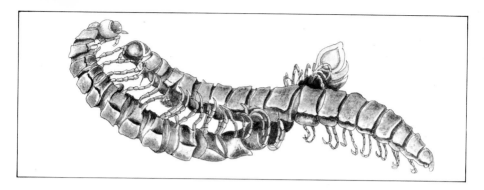

ments and limbs (see Figure 16). Symphyla are eyeless. They are much more common than pauropods in forest litter, and are very active. Although they do not burrow, they sometimes find their way down soil crevices to a depth of several centimetres – especially in summer when the soil is dry and in winter before it freezes. They feed mainly on plant detritus, leaf-mould, and dead moss, eating only the soft tissues, but may also attack living rootlets.

Millipedes

Although all millipedes are essentially animals of the soil, a broad distinction can be made between those millipedes which live mainly in woodland litter and those which can also penetrate more deeply into the ground. The millipedes of the litter layer tend to be flat-backed types (shown in Figure 18) and specialise in forcing their way into cracks between the layers of semi-decayed leaves on the forest floor, while soil millipedes are more often cylindrical in cross-section. The flat-backed Polydesmida are not only susceptible to drying up, but are also incapacitated by too much water. They are, therefore, ideally placed in the litter layer, which is secure from both drought and flooding. In contrast, the soil-dwelling Iulida are not subject to the same limitations and can move up or down the soil profile safely.

Millipedes feed mainly on dead vegetation

Figure 18   Flat-backed millipedes mating.

Figure 19   Pill millipede.

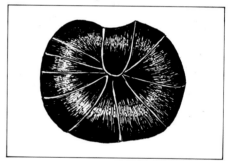

such as tree leaves, twigs or rotten wood; but some appear to prefer food with a higher content of nitrogen, such as fungal hyphae or dead animal matter. By virtue of the wider range of habitats available, the woodland floor supports more species of millipede than does the soil of any other habitat in the British Isles. The sizes of woodland populations have been estimated to be in the order of 50–150 individuals per square metre, but there is considerable scope for investigations of the numbers of millipedes in different types of woodland throughout Britain.

The well-known pill millipede (Figure 19) is a characteristic inhabitant of the leaf litter of beech woods on chalky soil in southern England. (Although often confused with the pill woodlouse, it can easily be distinguished from it by its glossy black colour and the shield-like plate behind the head, the presence of 17 pairs of legs, as opposed to 5 in the woodlouse, and the absence of small abdominal segments.) Together with some iulid millipedes, the pill millipede occupies a similar ecological niche to that of the larger burrowing species of earthworms. Both incorporate organic detritus on the soil surface with mineral material which they ingest with their food. Unlike earthworms, millipedes of this type are able to inhabit acid soils and shallow calcareous soils which do not retain much moisture. In localities such as these, millipedes rank first among the humus-forming organisms of the soil. They are, however, even more plentiful in alkaline soils, where they supplement the activities of worms.

Some millipedes, both flat-backed and cylindrical, climb up the vegetation of the herb layer and feed not on the foliage itself but on soft fruits, fungal hyphae and the like. Many are found underneath stones and loose bark, while the tiny, bristly millipede can sometimes be seen moving across the trunks of trees and emerging from beneath the lichen on rocks. How it manages to walk in the sunshine without becoming completely dried up is a complete mystery. Possibly its clothing of dense spines may trap a layer of damp air around is body, thereby slowing down the rate of evaporation.

Centipedes

Whereas in millipedes there are two pairs of legs to each body segment, centipedes have only one. Even so, some of the longest of the soil-dwelling Geophilomorpha may have more legs than the average millipede. Centipedes are carnivorous, feeding on a variety of small arthropods and molluscs, which they catch with their poison claws or modified first legs. It is possible that geophilomorphs may sometimes eat small worms, but it is doubtful whether large

worms are attacked. Whereas these long-bodied centipedes burrow into the earth, the shorter Lithobiomorpha are fast-running predatory inhabitants of litter and the under-surfaces of bark and stones; they sometimes climb the trunks of trees at night. Both kinds tend to lose water rapidly at low humidities and, like woodlice, are nocturnal and confined to damp environments for most of their lives.

In most species of Geophilomorpha, the number of pairs of legs varies from one individual to another, and females tend to have more than males of the same species. The number of pairs is, however, always odd. In contrast, Lithobiomorpha invariably have 15 pairs of legs and the sexes are similar in this respect. Male centipedes spin webs on which, after highly complex pre-mating behaviour, they deposit sperm droplets. The females are guided to these webs, both by the males and by the threads with which the webs are attached to the substrate and take up the sperm. Geophilomorphs lay their eggs in the soil, where the mother guards them until they hatch; but Lithobiomorpha deposit their eggs singly and cover them with earth. The eggs hatch into larvae which have fewer legs than the adults. The number of legs increases in subsequent moults.

Insects

The insects of British woodlands fall naturally into four ecological groups: soil and cryptozoic insects, which are mostly wingless (although, surprisingly, leaf litter often contains a number of small two-winged flies which have recently emerged from their pupae); bark- and wood-boring insects (mostly larvae); insects that live on the vegetation (including plant-sucking aphids and white flies, bush crickets, caterpillars, gall midges etc); and aerial insects. There is, naturally, considerable overlap between these groups. For example, insects that are not in flight frequently rest on the vegetation;

aphids sometimes take to wing; springtails are not confined to leaf litter but may often be found among vegetation; caterpillars that metamorphose into butterflies and moths forsake their diet of green leaves to become aerial nectar feeders, and so on.

Soil and cryptozoic insects

Vigorously leaping springtails, or Collembola, and speedy bristletails (Thysanura) – which are related to the domestic silverfish and firebrat – are conspicuous inhabitants of the cryptosphere. Whereas Collembola are also found among living foliage, Thysanura always live a concealed life in the soil or rotting wood, or under stones and fallen leaves; they are seldom to be seen unless disturbed. Collembola, today, are regarded by most workers as a separate arthropodan class, and are not classified as insects; but it is often convenient to treat them as such. They rarely exceed 2–3mm in length and are found in the soil, in decaying vegetable matter, under the bark of trees and among herbage. Some species inhabit the nests of ants. Collembola are saprophagous or phytophagous, feeding respectively on decaying materials and on pollen grains and fungal spores. A characteristic feature of their biology is a tendency to gregariousness, large numbers of individuals, both adult and immature, sometimes massing together. They form a basic item in the woodland food chain, being preyed on by other insects, small spiders and falsescorpions. Thysanura are likewise common in soil, in leaf deposits on the woodland floor, and some species also inhabit the nests of ants. Like springtails, they are an important item in forest food chains.

Earwigs Another group of soil-dwelling and cryptozoic insects is the Dermaptera or earwigs. Nocturnal in habit, they hide away in the soil, under bark and stones, or among herbage during the day. At night they emerge to feed on flower petals and tender foliage,

Glanville fritillary

as well as on dead and living insects. The common earwig seldom takes to the air, although it has well developed wings; but the lesser earwig flies quite frequently, even during the day. The name 'earwig' may have originated from the fact that these insects have occasionally been known to use the human ear as a place of concealment; but is is more likely that the word is a contraction of 'ear-wing', because the hind wings are shaped like the human outer ear. The characteristic forceps are primarily weapons of offence and defence. They are sometimes used in folding up the wings, and also play a part in mating. The female earwig deposits her eggs in an excavation that she has prepared below the surface of the soil, and remains on guard over them, as well as over the young for a short while after they have hatched. Because of this limited care of their young, earwigs are often called 'sub-social'.

Beetles The woodland soil and litter communities contain large numbers of beetles. Many species are uncommon, and are represented by only a few individuals, the total population being made up, in the main, of comparatively few common types. This fact can be related to the large number of minor habitats present within a small area of woodland, and with the diversity of food substances available. Some predatory ground beetles (Carabidae) are widespread, as are some Staphylinidae or rove beetles. Many of these woodland beetles are dark-coloured, which may be connected with their nocturnal habits. Species active in the daytime often have light metallic colours. The carabid life-cycle usually takes a year to complete. Some species become active early in the year, producing larvae which feed and grow during the summer months. The new adult generation emerges in the autumn and overwinters, becoming active during the following spring. Other species reproduce in the autumn, and overwinter as larvae which develop into adults the following spring. In this way competition between similar species may be reduced.

Ants Woodlands are inhabited by fewer species of ants than are more open habitats, and it is probably no coincidence that wood ants are the only ones that are able effectively to conserve their metabolic heat. Furthermore, their relatively large size enables them to walk the long distances between the tree tops, where they hunt for insects in the foliage, and their nests on the ground. Most ants build irregular, subterranean nests, throwing out the excavated earth to form mounds on the soil surface. The big wood ants of British forests, however, build large surface nests – a metre or more in height – of twigs, leaves, grass, pine needles or pebbles. Although widely distributed in England and parts of Scotland, they are rare in Ireland. Nests are made in shady places, in clearings and on the borders as well as in the interiors of woods and forests. Wood ants are usually associated with fir trees, but oak, birch and other woods are also colonised. Ants occur everywhere, but woods on chalk and sandy soil seem to be the most productive. Colonies can be found under stones, under bark and at the foot of trees, in stumps and fallen branches, in hollow trees, on banks, and even in the nests of other species of ant.

Despite the fact that ants are usually hostile to most living creatures, several other kinds of animals do succeed in living in the nests of ants. Some of these guests, or 'myrmecophiles', are symbiotic and of benefit to the ants. They include aphids, scale insects and other bugs. Others are more or less harmful lodgers, and a few are parasites of one kind or another. Many of the lodgers are beetles – usually belonging to the family Staphylinidae – which can be recognised by their very short elytra or wing-cases. The parasites of ants include mites, ichneumon wasps, flies and nematode worms. Predators include birds, toads and a few spiders.

Bark and wood boring insects

Among the numerous woodland insects with vegetarian habits are bark-feeders, wood-borers, seed-feeders, root-feeders and fungus-eaters. Bark-feeders are mostly beetles of the family Scolytidae, whose tunnels and galleries can be seen as elegant patterns when pieces of loose bark are stripped from the trunk of a dead elm. These are the insects which disperse the fungal pathogens responsible for the Dutch elm disease which has destroyed so many British elm trees in recent years.

The female beetle cuts a short entrance tunnel in the bark. This leads into the main gallery, which is first widened to form a pairing chamber where mating takes place. The female bark beetle then excavates the main gallery further, laying eggs in niches along its sides as she does so. When the larvae emerge, they gnaw side galleries extending at right angles to the main passage. As the larvae grow in size, the galleries gradually become deeper and wider, finally ending in pupal cells. The newly metamorphosed beetles gnaw their way directly outwards through the bark to the exterior of the tree.

Among other bark-feeders are the ash bark beetle, whose main gallery consists of two horizontal branches with the larval galleries short and spaced closely together, and the destructive pine weevil, which does most damage in the adult stages, since its larvae feed mainly on the stumps of felled trees.

Wood-boring insects include the larvae of large and handsome longicorn beetles. These larvae form an important item in the food of woodpeckers. Oaks, poplars and willows are the trees most frequently attacked by them. Conifers, on the other hand, are susceptible to the attentions of hornet-like wood wasps. The females of these splendid insects cannot sting – they use their stout, saw-like, ovipositors to drill holes into tree trunks where the eggs are laid. Many people are scared stiff of wood wasps because they look so dangerous, but they are completely harmless. The caterpillars of the goat moth, which have to eat a large quantity of wood in order to obtain sufficient nourishment, gnaw burrows large enough to admit a human finger.

The family Curculionidae (weevils) includes numerous seed-eating species, including the long-snouted nut weevils, whose larvae tunnel into hazelnuts and acorns. Root-feeders are mostly the larvae of beetles and flies, while the larvae of ambrosia beetles feed on the moulds which infect dead wood. Fungi are also eaten by the larvae of flies such as fungus gnats (Mycetophilidae) and small rove beetles.

Insects of the vegetation

The leaves of trees, shrubs and herbs provide the primary source of food for woodland insects. Some, such as aphids and white fly, obtain nourishment from sap which is sucked from the leaves and delicate stems of the vegetation. Others, such as the caterpillars of Lepidoptera and saw-flies, eat leaves. These digest the contents of plant cells (the cell walls and skeletal parts pass through their guts unchanged, for caterpillars have no enzymes capable of breaking down and utilising cellulose). Looper caterpillars (Geometridae), which have only two pairs of abdominal legs, are especially damaging to arboreal foliage, as are larvae that cause leaf-rolling. The green oak-roller moth (Tortricidae), for example, sometimes becomes so abundant in the older oak woods of southern England that trees are left bare over considerable areas of countryside. The larvae cause leaves to roll up, become shrivelled, and fall. Many woodland herbs are destroyed by saw-fly caterpillars. These also attack the young needles of pines, and sometimes defoliate entire plantations. Trees may be severely harmed by defoliators but, in Britain, are seldom killed in this way.

Larvae of tiny moths, as well as a few fly larvae, inhabit the narrow spaces between the upper and lower epidermis of leaves. As they burrow or mine, they make tracks of various shapes. Some of these are narrow, winding galleries; others appear as blotches on the leaves. Finally, galls may be produced by various kinds of organism, including eelworms, mites and insects. Ash trees, especially, are affected. Oak-apples are caused by one kind of gall wasp, while the spangle galls on the leaves of oaks are caused by gall wasps of another genus.

Insects do not eat leaves only in their larval stages. Both nymphs and adult bush crickets, or long-horned grasshoppers (Orthoptera), dwell among the leaves of trees and bushes. The females have broad, sword-like ovipositors which are used for cutting slits in stems and twigs, in which the eggs are laid, or for burying them deep in the soil. Some adult beetles, bugs (Hemiptera) and insects of various other orders may devour the foliage of woodland trees. There is even one small species of cicada to be found in the New Forest although, in general, the cicadas are insects of warmer climes than ours.

Aerial insects

Various kinds of flying insects thrive beneath the shelter of the trees. The orders most commonly encountered on the wing in forest and woodland are the Lepidoptera (butterflies and moths), Hymenoptera (bees, wasps and ichneumons) and Diptera (flies). Aquatic insects, including Odonata (dragonflies) and Trichoptera (caddis flies), appear in the vicinity of woodland ponds and streams.

Butterflies Woodland is the true home of many butterfly species. The small pearl-bordered fritillary is more common in northern Britain, whilst the large is more common in the south and is not found in the north of Scotland. Apparently the small requires damper environments than does the large pearl-bordered fritillary, and is not found in dry woods. It is extremely rare in Ireland. The high brown fritillary is a forest species of southern England and Wales, while the silver-washed fritillary is more wide-spread, especially to the west and in Ireland. Its special stronghold is the New Forest. The heath fritillary is really a woodland species also, living only in southern counties where cow-wheat grows.

The rare large tortoiseshell is an inhabitant of woods in which elm is common, but it is seldom found outside East Anglia. The common white admiral and purple emperor may sometimes be seen flying on the outskirts of larger woods but they have local distributions and do not occur throughout much of Britain. The purple hairstreak is not often observed in flight, because it normally frequents the higher branches of oak trees. Other woodland butterflies include the holly blue, chequered skipper and wood white – now all sadly reduced as more and more true

woodland (as opposed to individual trees) is destroyed for agricultural purposes.

Moths Moths can be distinguished from butterflies by the fact that although they may have many different types of antennae these never bear knobs on the end as do those of butterflies. Woodlands are the home of numerous species of moth, many of which possess concealing coloration so that they become inconspicuous when resting on leaves, lichen or the bark of trees. The distribution of woodland moths can be explained in relation to their food plants. The species that inhabit beech woods, for example, are coloured so that they harmonise with the colour of withered beech leaves, even if they are only distantly related to one another. Examples are afforded by the barred hook-tip and clay triple-lines. Oaks and deciduous woods have their own characteristic species, as do ash and yew trees, poplars and willows. The northern birch scrub supports the superb large emerald, grey birch and yellow horned moths, in addition to many other species that have become adapted to this distinct habitat.

Flies Flies are common woodland insects. Throughout most of the year, dancing swarms of midges perform their aerial gymnastics in forest clearings, rising together and falling in unison, while occasionally a mating pair leaves the others and flutters to the ground. The popular name of 'winter gnats' has been earned for the family Trichoceridae on account of the habit of congregating in dancing swarms in midwinter. They may appear in the forest in quite cold weather and are often to be seen as the wintry sun is setting and the atmosphere is still – sometimes even when snow lies on the ground. Unlike mosquitoes, which can be a menace in woodland, winter gnats do not bite. Even less attractive to all except perhaps the more devoted naturalist are the horseflies and clegs (Tabanidae) which infest open spaces in woods. These stoutly built insects include our largest blood-sucking flies. The biggest species are mostly confined to old forest areas such as the New Forest. Their approach may be heralded by a deep, soft, hum; some, however, betray their presence only by the sharp prick of their bite. The clegs, in particular, are very persistent in their attacks, even after being driven away again and again. They can be recognised by their smaller size and mottled wings. The larger species are really beautiful insects, with large, iridescent eyes, whose colour fades after death. Only the females suck blood. Moisture appears to be essential for breeding, larvae occurring in ditches, ponds, moist soil, rotting wood and similar places.

The so-called 'forest fly' belongs to the family of louse-flies and is an ectoparasite of deer and ponies in the New Forest and other wooded regions. After flying to their host,

these unattractive insects lose their wings and assume a louse-like mode of life. When they move rapidly sideways, like an anxious crab, clinging to the skin of the host, they create a most unpleasant sensation which may cause horses that are unaccustomed to them to bolt. However, their bites seem to cause little irritation to the ponies and cattle of the forest, which have become acquainted with these parasites.

A walk through the forest at any season of the year, except winter, is sure to produce an encounter with hoverflies (Syrphidae), suspended and apparently stationary in the air yet able to dart forwards, backwards or sideways, with equal agility. They can be seen in glades and footpaths, where they often shine like little jewels in the shafts of sunlight that pierce the tracery of the leaves. These lovely insects, remarkable for their powers of hovering, are usually brightly coloured and may be striped, spotted or banded with yellow on a metallic blue or black ground colour. This often

Orb-web of argiopid spider

imparts to them a superficial resemblance to wasps. Nearly all the members of this family are attracted to the flowers of the forest and hover above them. Their larval habits are extremely varied. Some syrphid larvae are predatory, preying upon aphids and other plant-sucking bugs; others may be plant-eaters or saprophytes, living on decaying organic matter, dung, mud, dirty water, rotting wood, and so on.

Arachnids

Woodland and forest undoubtedly provide the richest environment for spiders, false-scorpions and harvestmen in the British Isles. This is because they present such a wide diversity of microhabitats, to each of which different species are adapted. Woodland spiders can be divided into three main ecological groupings: ground-living hunting spiders, the spiders that live in foliage and vegetation, and aerial web-spinners. The third category does not apply to false-scorpions and harvestmen.

False-scorpions

Except that they lack a caudal sting, false-scorpions resemble tiny scorpions. The most primitive of British arachnids, they seldom measure more than 3·5mm in length, and few species attain even this size. Because they are so small and have shy, retiring habits, pseudoscorpions are little known and seldom found unless specially sought. This is a pity, for they are interesting creatures and many aspects of their biology provide suitable subjects for study by both amateur and professional zoologists.

Most pseudoscorpions avoid the light and do not often venture into the open. They may be collected by hand from rotting leaves and from under the bark of trees, but this method tends to be laborious, for they are by no means plentiful. The most effective method entails the use of a heated funnel, but a simpler way is to scatter fallen leaves, moss and other vegetable debris onto a sheet of newspaper or a white table top. Despite their small size, the creatures can then be easily recognised by their squarish shape. They generally crouch motionless, their legs and chelae drawn in until they are touched, when they at once proclaim their nature by running backwards. False-scorpions walk slowly with an air of impressive dignity and calm deliberation which distinguishes them from most of the other small arthropods that inhabit the same type of locality, their enormous pedipalps spread out in front of them like the antennae of an insect. If, as they proceed, they happen to touch some other animal with the long hairs on their extended palps, they dart sideways or backwards with surprising speed, looking rather like a startled crayfish. This sudden retreat is highly characteristic, for not many animals can go backwards as easily as forwards, and very few more rapidly.

False-scorpions are found in a variety of woodland habitats, different species occurring in soil, in decaying vegetation, on the under-surfaces of logs and stones, and in moss and humus. Quite a number of species are myrmecophilous, and live in the nests of ants. They also occur in birds' nests in hollow trees, and some cling to the legs of flies, thereby obtaining transport from one place to another. Exclusively carnivorous, pseudoscorpions feed on Collembola, Symphyla, small insects and spiders, which may be poisoned by the secretion of glands in the claws.

Mating is complex, sometimes involving courtship dances and displays before the sperm-packet, or spermatophore, is deposited by the male and taken up into the genitalia of the female. The males of some woodland species that inhabit damp leaf litter, however, produce spermatophores in isolation and the females take them up when they come across them. This kind of sperm transfer is primitive, wasteful and effective only when there are comparatively large populations of false-scorpions. The eggs may be retained beneath

the abdomen of the mother, enclosed in a transparent membrane and nourished by a milky fluid. In these species, the females construct brood nests and remain in them until the young are ready to disperse. In some, the newly emerged nymphs ride on their mothers' backs, as baby scorpions do.

Above Zebra spider

Right Wolf-spider, with egg sac.

Below Sparassid hunting spider

Spiders

During spring and early summer, the carpet of dead leaves beneath the trees is continually enlivened by the restless movements of innumerable wolf spiders, or Lycosidae, which, when still, are camouflaged by their dark-brown bodies – until they are disturbed by approaching footsteps. These active predators are the most obvious of the ground-hunting spiders. They lead a wandering existence, without any permanent retreats, carrying their egg-sacs fastened to the spinnerets. When the baby spiderlings hatch out, they mount their mothers' backs, where they remain clustered until after their first moult. During this time they do not feed, but exist on the nourishment obtained from digesting the remains of the embryonic yolk.

Wolf spiders have relatively good eyesight. They creep up to their prey then leap on it and kill it with a quick bite. If necessary, they will chase an insect for some distance before making the kill. Because they hunt their prey by sight, and it is necessary for the male spider to be recognised for what he is by the larger and more powerful female, courting wolf spiders indulge in visual displays. These have the effect of blocking the hunger drive of the females, and suppressing their predatory instincts. Each species of wolf spider has its own distinct courtship display. In many, the male raises his forelegs, displaying their darker segments, and stretches forward with his enlarged feelers or pedipalps. Numerous variations of this form of signalling have been described in different wolf spiders, each of which is only effective in influencing females of the same species as the male.

Related to the wolf spiders is a family known as Pisauridae, of which one species is extremely common in woods, ditches, herbaceous vegetation and such places. Comparatively large (reaching a length of up to 15mm), with a tapering abdomen, its prevailing colour ranges from light grey to rich brown, with a pale stripe in the centre of the carapace and an abdominal pattern of dark spots bordered by wavy lines. Female Pisauridae carry their egg-sacs in their jaws, but still connected by threads to the spinnerets. When the eggs are ready to hatch, the cocoon is attached to a blade of grass; the mother weaves a tent over it, and remains on guard outside until the young have hatched and dispersed. During their first instar, while they are still absorbing the embryonic yolk, the little spiderlings cluster together inside their tent. After moulting, however, they go their separate ways and the mother is released from her vigil.

Other common hunting spiders of British woodlands belong to the families Gnaphosidae and Clubionidae. These are mostly short-sighted nocturnal predators which spend the daylight hours in silken cells under bark, logs and stones. Most of them are uniformly grey, brown or black, and they detect their prey by the sense of touch. They are extremely ferocious and will feed on other species of spider as readily as on insects. Mating takes place in April, but the sexes remain together for some months afterwards. The male courts his dangerous wife with trembling legs, daring to enter her cell only if she does not rattle her body and snap at him when he comes near.

One very dramatic nocturnal ground-hunting spider, belonging to the family Dysderidae (Figure 19), can be recognised immediately by its brick-red carapace and legs, and the pale yellow abdomen. The day is passed in a silken cell beneath bark and stones, or amongst thick clumps of vegetation, whence the spider emerges at night in search of its prey – woodlice – for the destruction of which the enormous jaws are evidently adapted. When the sexes meet, they feel and caress each other with their legs, whose sinuous movements convey the information that predation would not be an appropriate conclusion to the encounter.

Galls on ash tree.

Two families of spider are typical inhabitants of leaves and foliage. These are the jumping spiders, or Salticidae, and the crab spiders (Thomisidae). The behaviour of jumping spiders is even more attuned to vision than is that of wolf spiders – as attested by their large eyes and alert demeanour. Jumping spiders usually leave their retreats and hunt for prey while the sun is shining. When they see an insect, they approach stealthily and capture it with a sudden leap. The well-known zebra spider, recognisable by its black and white stripes, can often be found hunting on walls, fences and tree trunks. As it walks along, it fastens a safety thread or dragline at intervals to the surface on which it is moving. Extension of the legs is achieved by a sudden increase in blood pressure, caused in

turn by the contraction of the dorso-ventral muscles of the thorax. The jump is controlled by the safety thread, which is paid out from the spinnerets. If this happens to break, the spider tumbles head over heels, like a kite whose string has been released. Many of the jumping spiders are brightly coloured and their elaborate courtship dances and visual displays were the first examples of such behaviour to have been described in spiders.

Unlike the hunting spiders discussed so far, crab spiders (Thomisidae) do not stalk or chase their prey. Instead, they lie in wait and, as it passes unawares, seize it with the two front pairs of legs, which are unusually strong and no doubt specially adapted for this purpose. Like crabs, these little spiders often run sideways and, when at rest awaiting the arrival of prey, sit with their legs spread out to their sides. Most species have broad, flattened, colourful bodies which match their backgrounds. Some wait among the petals of flowers, where their light hues help to make them inconspicuous, and a few are even able to change colour so that they match their background. Visiting insects are seized by the waiting spiders as they alight on the flowers in search of nectar. Some crab spiders that inhabit the herb layer of the woodland vegetation are long and thin, and these stretch their legs fore and aft as they lie on the blades of grass. Their green coloration renders them extremely inconspicuous – both to predators and to their prey. Mating in crab spiders is an unusual business. In some kinds the male binds his mate to the ground with silk threads, and fertilises her before she has extricated herself. As in all spiders, the adult male deposits seminal fluid on a special sperm web, absorbs it with his enlarged palps or feelers and, in mating, applies these to the female's genitalia. Mature male spiders can always be recognised as such by the large bulbs at the ends of their pedipalps.

Some types of woodland trees and shrubs harbour far more spiders than others do. The

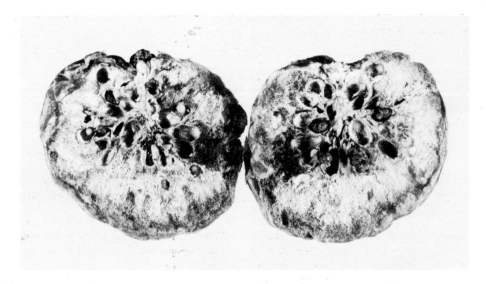

Oak apple gall cut in two to show larval gall wasps inside.

foliage of alder, willow and beech trees, for example, is inhabited by fewer individuals representing fewer species than that of oak, box, holly, yew and conifers. Certain plants of the herb and shrub layers, such as grasses, heather and gorse, are likewise more richly endowed with a fauna of spiders than are bluebells, bracken and laurel. This may be due to a number of factors. Some plants are more attractive to the insects on which spiders prey than others are; some provide firmer support for the attachment of webs; some maintain a higher humidity in their foliage, while others provide more shelter from the wind.

Some web-spinning spiders, as well as hunting spiders, inhabit the layer of leaf litter on the woodland floor, cracks and holes in tree trunks, rotting logs, and so on. Spiders of the family Dictynidae betray their presence by their webs of ragged, bluish silk, emanating from the hole down which the spider lives. Agelenid spiders spin cobwebs among vegetation, similar to the cobwebs that decorate the corners of attics, garden houses and

potting sheds. Gorse is particularly favoured by these long-legged spiders. Dictynid webs, like those of the Agelenidae, are especially adapted for the capture of crawling and low-flying insect prey. Four families of British woodland spiders – the Theridiidae or comb-footed spiders, the orb-web builders (Argiopidae and Tetragnathidae) and the Linyphiidae or 'money spiders' – use aerial webs to capture winged prey in flight. These families include the most highly evolved of all British spiders. The suggestion has been made that predation by primitive spiders during the Carboniferous period engendered the evolution of insect wings; then, when their prey took to the air, spiders evolved aerial webs as a means of capturing them in flight. This is not, however, generally accepted.

The comb-footed spiders are usually small, often gaily coloured, and live mostly among the leaves of shrubs and bushes, where they spin their irregular webs. They have a characteristic comb on the tarsal segments of their fourth legs, with which they draw out a ribbon of silk to be thrown over their captives. Orb-web builders are the most highly specialised of all spider families. They

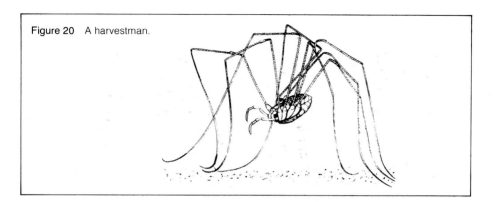

Figure 20   A harvestman.

detect their prey through the vibrations caused by its struggles in the web. In his courtship, therefore, the male taps out a coded message on the female's web so that she does not mistake him for prey. The 'money spiders' or Linyphiidae are by far the largest of the British spider families. Their characteristic sheet webs, beneath which the owners hang upside down, are to be found in almost every woodland shrub or tree. Unfortunately most species are extremely difficult to identify.

Harvestmen

Although distinct from spiders (Araneae), harvestmen or harvest spiders (Opiliones) are likewise an important element in the woodland fauna. Their bodies are oval (see Figure 20), and there is no narrow waist between the thorax and abdomen as in spiders, while the legs of most species are disproportionately long. Indeed, the long legs have a tactile function and enable their owners to detect suitable prey over quite a distance. They are really the equivalent of a mobile web, for harvestmen are formidable predators and have a varied diet. Some species climb the trunks of trees at night in search of food, others wander over the floor of the forest. Harvestmen tend to be more sensitive to desiccation than spiders. There is no courtship. The male has a penis of surprising length, which is inserted into the genital opening of the female, and mating lasts but a few seconds. The eggs are laid in batches in the soil or under logs and stones during the autumn. Most species live for about a year.

Mites

Although by no means conspicuous, on account of their small size, mites, or Acari, are among the most common soil animals throughout the country and are particularly abundant in woodland and forests that are rich in leaf litter and other organic material. The mites form a large and diverse group of arachnids. In the main, soil mites belong to one of four orders. They include both detritus-feeding and predatory forms, as well as species that feed on fungi, algae, bacteria, dung and the liquefied products of decomposition. Larger mites are more plentiful in the litter and upper layers of the soil; smaller species at greater depths. Like springtails, Acari differ in their ability to tolerate various environmental factors such as the level of moisture, and the organic content and possibly the acidity of the soil and litter. Some species have a very restricted distribution; others have a wide tolerance and a correspondingly widespread distribution.

Beetle mites (Oribatei) (see Figure 21) are probably the kind most often noticed by naturalists. They owe their popular name to the strong, dark-coloured armour that

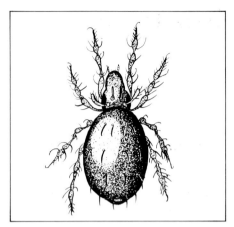

Figure 21   Beetle mite.

protects their bodies, and can easily be discerned by the naked eye as they crawl among twigs and fallen leaves. They are vegetarians, feeding to a considerable extent upon fungi growing in the cryptosphere. Most soil mites, however, are soft, pale creatures, although a few are scarlet in colour. Among the latter are the harvest mites or jiggers, found mainly on chalky soils. During the autumn, these burrow into the human skin, causing intense irritation.

The basic life-cycle of soil Acari consists of development from an egg into a six-legged larval stage, followed by from one to three stages as an eight-legged nymph, and finally the adult form. Red-spider mites, well known as orchard pests, spend the winter as eggs that are bright red in colour. These are laid on branches and twigs, and hatch in spring into larvae, which pass through various nymphal stages to the adult. Depending upon latitude and climate, there may be a number of generations during the course of the summer, the eggs hatching in about eight to ten days. Overwintering eggs are laid in the autumn, their production being triggered by the decreasing length of daylight. Cold weather then kills the adult mites, or causes the leaves on which they are feeding to fall.

The interrelationship of the widely diverse and incredibly numerous invertebrate animals discussed in this chapter with both the vegetation which supports them and the vertebrates that prey on them will be considered in the final chapter of this book.

5 Birds and mammals

The woodland community includes numerous vertebrate animals. Some of them are highly specialised and adapted to living in trees; others are 'generalists' which thrive in open country as well as they do in forest. The adaptations of animals to arboreal life are far less marked in temperate than in tropical forest, possibly because deciduous woodland is more broken up and diverse than equatorial and seasonal rain forest. In some arboreal birds, such as woodpeckers, the outermost toe has been rotated backwards so that this and the hallux, or big toe, oppose the second and third toes (as in all birds, there is no fifth toe). This arrangement gives a very firm grasp. The rotation is permanent in woodpeckers, but owls can turn their outermost toes forwards or backwards whenever they wish.

Most woodland mammals are terrestrial in habit, and only a few species are adapted to life in the trees. No temperate forest mammal has prehensile feet with opposable digits, or a prehensile tail like that of a spider monkey; but the claws are well developed in both squirrels and cats, and these animals cling tenaciously. Squirrels are truly arboreal in habit, and are 'branch runners' like the majority of other tree-dwelling mammals. They live and progress on all fours on the upper surfaces of the branches. Many other woodland mammals, including carnivores and rodents, are quite capable of climbing, although they do not show very marked adaptations for this. Birds and bats are the only vertebrates able to fly. Gliding forms, such as the flying squirrel of northern Europe, do not occur in the British Isles.

Amphibians and reptiles

The natterjack toad, the sand lizard, and its predator the smooth snake are restricted to sandy habitats and heathland. Consequently they do not occur in woods and forests –

Above Adder, or viper.

Below Slow worms are legless lizards.

except where there are large clearings and open spaces, as, for instance, in the New Forest. In contrast, the common toad, newts and frogs, the common lizard, the slow worm (really a legless lizard), the grass snake and the adder are widely dispersed throughout much of the British Isles wherever suitable conditions prevail. They may all be encountered in woodland, although this does not appear to be their favourite environment. For amphibians require open water for breeding, and many ponds and ditches in agricultural land have been drained and filled up; in many areas, village ponds, too, are a thing of the past. So the herpetologist may find Britain's undisturbed woodlands increasingly important places in which to study amphibians and reptiles. Both grass snakes and adders can sometimes be seen sunning themselves in forest glades, while newts and frogs enjoy the cool shade and damp grass beneath the trees.

Snakes are efficient predators, but their overall impact on the woodland community appears to be slight. Although some small rodents form an important item in the diet of adders, for example, it seems unlikely that adders alone noticeably reduce rodent populations. Lizards and frogs feed on insects and other arthropods, as well as on worms and slugs. They are themselves preyed on by a number of vertebrates. Adult frogs are eaten by grass snakes, hawks, owls, crows, hedgehogs, weasels, rats, otters, badgers and stoats; lizards are eaten by adders more often than by grass snakes, and by blackbirds, shrikes, kestrels, buzzards and weasels. When shrews meet lizards while hunting, they actively avoid contact with the reptiles.

Lizards and snakes may sometimes be captured for study using a stick or a fishing rod with an inconspicuous noose attached. With care, it is possible to slide the noose over the head of the reptile, then jerk it up and thus capture the animal. Lizards are not as wary of a thread or fishing line and a stick as they are of a human being. This collecting technique is difficult to use successfully in thick undergrowth, however, or when the wind is strong and gusty. Care should, of course, be exercised in handling the poisonous adder – indeed, it is better to leave adders severely alone and merely to take photographs of them with a telephoto lens. Another method of capturing lizards is by means of a strong rubber band which is flicked at them like a catapult. It is usually possible to run up and catch them before they recover from the surprise and shock. They are not in any way harmed by this treatment.

Birds

The insects that flourish in the relatively humid forest environment provide an excellent source of food for birds. It is not by chance, therefore, that most woodland birds of temperate regions are insectivorous. In contrast, since tropical rain forest trees and shrubs flower or fruit throughout the year, the proportion of frugivorous and seed-eating birds is much higher in the tropics than it is in the British Isles. In Britain, some species of birds avoid the winter altogether by migrating, while others must become omnivorous if they are to survive the season in which insect life is largely dormant. When invertebrate life almost disappears at the onset of winter, the blue tit, for example, has to spend almost all its time searching for items of food. Furthermore, the hours of daylight are reduced, and the tit's small size and correspondingly large surface to volume ratio make it especially susceptible to cold. The mortality of blue tits is heavy in hard winters because these little birds often do not find enough food to generate the metabolic heat necessary to keep them warm.

In mild weather, the blackbird and song thrush are able to drag bulky and nutritious earthworms from the ground. But a sharp frost may make the soil impenetrable, and then only a meagre supply of soft berries

Tree-creeper

remains between them and starvation. Woodpeckers, hammering away at a stout tree to reach the wood-boring insects on which they feed, may seem to have evolved a laborious method of feeding. Its advantage only becomes apparent in freezing weather, when spotted woodpeckers do not seem to suffer to any appreciable extent. The green woodpecker, however, is somewhat more susceptible, because it depends almost as much on ground-living ants as it does on wood-boring insects. Consequently, when anthills are frozen so hard that the woodpecker's bill cannot penetrate them, an important source of food is lost just at the time when it is most needed. Specialisation conveys both advantages and disadvantages. The slender, curved bill of the tree-creeper is adapted so that its owner can reach insects and other cryptozoans hiding in bark crevices. The bird works upward from the base of a tree, running spirally up the bole as it searches for its food. Then it flies to the base of another tree and begins again. Although the tree-creeper's beak is so well adapted for capturing cryptozoic insects, it is inefficient for taking flying insects, while a swallow or flycatcher, specialising on such food, cannot find the cryptozoic animals on which the tree-creeper survives throughout the winter and is, therefore, compelled to migrate to warmer climes.

Long-tailed tit

Dietary adaptations

As already indicated, the basic food of woodland birds consists of seeds and invertebrate animals. Since both of these are dependent on the plant cover, bird life is naturally determined, to a considerable extent, by the species and age of the trees. Some kinds of birds may be found in different types of woodland; others are specialised for life in more restricted habitats. For instance, the crested tit is seldom seen away from Scots pines, while the crossbill is largely confined to coniferous woods. Different bird species may require different habitats within a wood, and their presence and numbers are influenced by environmental factors, such as the existence of understorey vegetation to provide shelter, nesting sites, perches, etc. The presence of dead trees and fallen branches is another important factor. The number of woodland birds has been found to increase considerably when nesting boxes are installed in forest plantations. This indicates that populations of hole-nesting species, such as titmice and the pied flycatcher, are controlled mainly by the existence of suitable nesting sites.

Just as the trunks and branches of trees are explored by tree-creepers – and, in a different way, by woodpeckers – so are the twigs, stalks and leaves searched by various titmice. At the same time, birds like the brambling and chaffinch breed in woodland when food is abundant. Every part of the wood is exploited by one or more species of birds, no two species overlapping exactly in their requirements and way of life. Most insectivorous birds that do not migrate to areas where insects remain active feed on seeds during the winter; but tits and tree-creepers remain in deciduous forest throughout the year and survive the winter by finding insect larvae and pupae. They have such specialised habits and food preferences that the different species can live together without competing too strongly with one another. The blue tit is very light in weight, quick and agile, with a delicate bill – adapted for feeding in swaying trees. In contrast, the great tit is more heavily built and has a stout beak more suited to sheltered shrubs where seeds and berries are plentiful. The coal tit is most numerous in coniferous woodland, where the great tit and marsh tit are scarce, while the blue tit and long-tailed tit are widely distributed, although the former occupies lower strata of the vegetation, as shown in Figure 22.

Figure 22 (right) Feeding sites of tits. Although from time to time they may feed in similar sites, the different species of tits tend to hunt in different places. The great tit, in particular, is too heavy to be able to search the small twigs like the blue and coal tits.

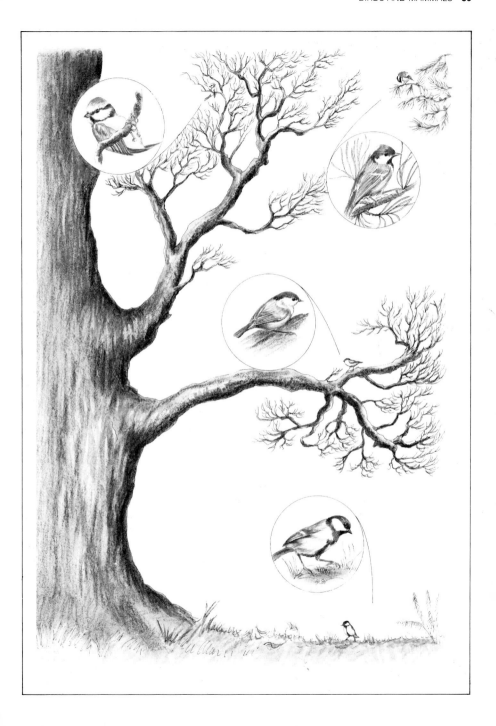

Figure 23 Crossbill showing crossed mandibles.

The nuthatch collects acorns and hazelnuts, carries them to a crevice which acts as a vice, hammers them with its stout beak and eats the contents after their shells have been broken. The hawfinch, likewise, is adapted to feeding on kernels and seeds and, to crack a cherry stone, can exert a force equivalent to a weight of 30–40kg at the tip of its beak. It spends most of its life in the trees, and is seldom seen on the ground except in winter, when it feeds on fallen seeds. Crossbills are completely adapted to life in coniferous woodland. They live in the upper branches of the trees like little parrots, which they resemble somewhat with their gay plumage. Their beaks are specially modified to split fir-cones, the upper and lower mandibles being crossed so that the tips overlap (Figure 23). Rooks, crows and magpies are omnivorous, and will feed readily on fruit, grain, eggs, insects, small birds, mammals and carrion. Their versatility and intelligence enable them to survive the winter without migrating.

Bird habitats

Natural selection has been in operation ever since the origin of life, and there can be few animal characteristics that are not adaptive in one way or another, although their purpose may not be immediately obvious. Many of these adaptations must be related to the environment or environments that animals inhabit. The woodland bird community comprises birds which roost or nest in woods but feed outside them, those which feed in the trees and shrubs, and those which feed on the ground. The jackdaw, rook, starling, woodpigeon and finches are examples of the first group; the titmice, spotted woodpecker and most of the migrants of the second; the blackbird, thrush and – if herbage is included with the ground – the wren are examples of the third.

The avifauna of woodland can also be subdivided vertically. For example, the wren, great tit, blue tit and woodpigeon occupy the herb, shrub, tree and upper canopy levels respectively (see Figure 22). The observant naturalist can add greatly to his understanding of the woodland bird community by noting the levels at which he sees different species, as he ticks them off on his checklist.

Every type of woodland has its characteristic bird population. Species that are common nearly everywhere include the jay, magpie, crow, blue tit, great tit, chaffinch, song thrush, woodpigeon and blackbird. The richest diversity of bird life is found in oak woods with their rich variety of trees and underlying vegetation. Here blue tits predominate over great tits, especially in autumn and winter, while there may be immigrations of long-tailed tits during the summer. Tit flocks begin to form in June and July. These are composed mainly of younger birds – many of the older blue tits and great tits maintain

Spotted flycatcher

their territories throughout the year. In winter nuthatches associate with the flocks of tits, together with goldcrests and tree-creepers, while willow warblers join them for a short while during the autumn. Willow warblers are really scrubland birds and are more abundant in woods where the under-storey of hazel and hawthorn is particularly well developed. Chiffchaffs occur where there is space for feeding and suitable song posts. They usually breed in dense oak woods, but leave them after the nesting season. Song thrushes are not found in dense woodland, because they need open spaces for feeding. Consequently, they occur mainly in thin woodland or near the edges of the woods. Unlike blackbirds, thrushes do not turn over fallen leaves in search of food and are therefore more vulnerable to frosty weather.

Spotted flycatchers frequent open glades, whereas nightingales are found only where the undergrowth is dense. Stock doves nest in holes in older trees and in the forks of branches, while woodpigeons are found in all woods, feeding in open ground or, where that is not possible, in the canopy. Tawny owls are more frequent, especially where there are plenty of older trees with suitable holes for nesting. Jackdaws also nest in tree-holes and feed in open country, although they may enter forests in summer to eat the moth caterpillars which are then defoliating the oak trees. Green and greater spotted woodpeckers are found in open woodland of all kinds, but lesser spotted woodpeckers occur predomi-nantly in broad-leaved woods.

Wood warblers nest on the ground, where there is sufficient light for grass to grow. They feed in the canopy and sing in the lower branches of beech woods. Jays, marsh tits, hawfinches, chaffinches, bramblings, wood-pigeons and nuthatches feed on beech-mast, central Europe and parts of southern Europe, their numbers are dependent upon the crops of spruce cones. When these are scarce, they tend to wander. Occasionally large numbers of them irrupt into western Europe, especially France and Britain. An invasion of crossbills into England was chronicled by Matthew Paris in 1251.

Seasonal changes

As a wood passes through the successive stages of development to maturity, its bird fauna also changes. When heathland in south-eastern England is planted with conifers, the skylarks, meadow pipits, wheatears, stonechats and yellow wagtails characteristic of open country are gradually replaced by chaffinches, thrushes, wrens and hedge sparrows. After about fifteen years most of the heath species disappear, and true woodland birds – including the coal tit, blue tit, great tit, goldcrest, robin and jay – take over. Some 50 species of birds have been recorded in well established pine woods, but less than 20 actually breed there; the remainder nest in rides and open spaces, or even outside the pine stands, which they use only for roosting and feeding. Seasonal changes in the bird fauna also occur: chaffinches, greenfinches, goldfinches and bramblings move into pine plantations in the spring, when pine seeds become available for food. Although some competition for food must occur, in general the different insectivorous bird species tend to use different parts of a wood, some taking insects from the foliage of the trees, others from trunks and branches, or from the leaf litter beneath.

The number of species sheltering in a wood and feeding outside it is comparatively small, because trees and shrubs produce more food than does the ground and herbage. Many parts of a tree are edible, but the largest concentrations of protein are found in the buds and seeds, which between them provide a source of food throughout the year. Buds are es-

Greenfinch

when available. In lightly wooded heathland tree pipits are common and nightjars may also be found. Wood and willow warblers, siskins and lesser redpolls are characteristic species. The latter feed on birch catkins. Long-tailed tits, which – like willow warblers – are mainly birds of scrub, invade woodland in flocks after nesting in the open ground beyond. In pine woods, where there is little undergrowth, coal tits, goldcrests and treecreepers are to be found. Wood warblers are occasionally seen in dense pine plantations, but they usually prefer some secondary undergrowth. Crossbills are winter visitors to mature pine forests and sometimes breed in Britain after 'irruptions'. Normally nesting in the coniferous forests of Scandinavia, and in pecially valuable in winter and early spring when other foods are scarce; seeds and berries are the harvest of autumn and winter; insects are most abundant in summer. Many woodland birds and mammals follow an annual pattern of feeding, eating mainly buds in spring, insects in summer when the young are being reared, and seeds in the autumn and winter. Such a cycle is typical of the various British finches.

Economic importance

The capercaillie and black grouse eat young conifer shoots in winter. Starlings may roost in such numbers that they break the branches of trees. Woodpeckers make holes in trees already damaged by insects, and many birds eat the seeds of trees. Nevertheless, woodland birds are considered to inflict insignificant damage to the trees among which they live. On the other hand, birds assist in the dispersal of tree seeds. Succulent fruits, such as those of the yew, are eaten. The seeds pass undigested through the alimentary canal of the bird, to germinate where they are excreted. Jays feed on acorns, burying others that germinate more readily than those which lie on the surface of the ground. Many of the insects eaten by woodland birds are harmful to trees. It has been estimated that up to half of the insect larvae beneath the bark of a tree may be eaten by woodpeckers during the winter, and the frequency of insect attacks on forest trees can be reduced by installing nest boxes so that the density of the titmouse population is increased.

Control of insect pests by woodland birds is probably most effective during the winter, when populations are low and there is less other food available. Once an outbreak of pests has begun, however, birds are unable to control the insects because their numbers are too few. Only ichneumons and other parasitoids, nematodes, protozoans, bacteria, viruses, and other small disease-carrying organisms can reproduce fast enough to compete with the rapid rate of reproduction of pest insects. Birds of prey, such as owls and sparrowhawks, are truly beneficial to woodland and forest. They control the wood mice and voles which otherwise prevent the regeneration of the trees. Indeed, when all predatory birds have been removed by gamekeepers intent upon raising unnaturally large populations of pheasants the production of young trees is completely halted. This is because so many of the seeds are eaten by small rodents that no regeneration can take place. The prey selected by raptatory birds depends upon the vegetation cover. Rodents are eaten mainly in winter and spring, when ground cover is sparse. Later in the year, rabbits, rats and young moles become the main food of hawks and owls.

Mammals

The typical resident mammals of British woodlands include deer, squirrels, wood mice, martens and wild cats. The more striking forms are ground dwellers such as red and roe deer. Badgers and foxes are most at home along the forest margin; water voles and otters near water. Squirrels and bats make up the arboreal mammals. In olden times, bears, beavers, wild boars and wolves were also present, while the aurochsen hid their young in coverts as they grazed in the clearings of the forest. The relatively small number of tree species in Britain is less critical for vertebrates than it is for other animals, although some birds and mammals of temperate deciduous woodlands are absent from coniferous forests, and vice versa.

Insectivores

The Insectivora is the most primitive order of mammals to be found in Britain. It includes the shrews, the mole and the hedgehog, all of which inhabit woodland and forest. Shrews are easily recognised by their narrow, pointed snouts. They feed almost exclusively on insects, worms and snails, turning over dead

Cock pheasant

leaves and the surface soil with their snouts. Their surface to volume ratio is so great that they need to feed nearly all the time in order to keep themselves warm, and they do not hibernate in winter. Their soft velvet fur enables them to pass through the soil without getting dirty. The pygmy shrew is the smallest of all British mammals. It is widely distributed throughout the country, but lives mostly in wooded districts. It is an excellent climber, and somewhat less nocturnal in habits than the common shrew. Moreover, it never constructs its own runways through the ground vegetation, but moves in those of other animals, including common shrews. Nevertheless, direct competition between the two species seems to be avoided. In Ireland, where the common shrew is not found, its place is taken by the pygmy – although this species is never so abundant there as the common shrew is in England, Scotland and Wales.

From the latter part of summer onwards, dead shrews are frequently to be found throughout the countryside, usually without any signs of maltreatment, such as the marks of teeth and claws. Various explanations for this are discussed by Ron Freethy in *Man and Beast*. He points out that the bodies are most often seen in late summer and early autumn, when the shrew population is at its highest. It is possible that predators catch many shrews at this time but, finding the flesh unpalatable, leave the bodies uneaten. Shrews have a musky odour and neither cats nor dogs will eat them; but owls levy a heavy toll, as can be deduced from the contents of their pellets; and kestrels, magpies, jackdaws, stoats and vipers also take considerable numbers. Shrews are beneficial to mankind because they eat large quantities of insects, many of which are injurious to trees and agricultural plants.

The engineering works of moles are usually far more evident than the animals themselves. The mole's nest is located beneath a molehill, often hidden under a bramble or placed near a tree stump. It consists of an oval chamber containing a bed of dead leaves surrounded by dry grass from which extend a number of galleries leading to the mole's hunting grounds. In 1803, Antoine Cadet de Vaux described the mole's home as a 'fortress' consisting of a central chamber surrounded by two galleries, one above the other, and connected by five equidistant passages. Architectural plans and elevations, based on this description, were reproduced uncritically for over a century. In fact, a molehill is no more a fortress than is the nest of any other animal – although there is frequently an escape gallery which also serves to drain the nest.

In the past mole pelts were much appreciated by furriers because of a unique feature of the fur. Whichever way you stroke a mole, its fur always lies flat – an adaptation to living in narrow tunnels and moving along them both backwards and forwards. The storage of earthworms by the mole has been described by several writers. It seems that

Common shrew

surplus worms are bitten at the head end and thus immobilised before being stored in the walls of the tunnel. The mole is a slave to his appetite and, if kept without food, dies of starvation within a few hours. In addition to worms, wireworms and other destructive soil insects are eaten. Nevertheless, moles have traditionally been regarded as pests and persecuted by man. Their influence on the woodland ecosystem is, however, probably slight.

The original home of the hedgehog, formerly known as the 'urchin', was among the leaf litter of Britain's post-glacial forests. As these were gradually felled, and the resulting fields ploughed and enclosed by hedges, the animal established itself in the new environment and earned its new name. Until the beginning of the fifteenth century it had been known as 'il', which is a diminutive of the word 'Igel', its present-day name in German.

Hedgehogs are nocturnal creatures, spending the day under heaps of dead leaves or moss and emerging at night to eat worms, insects, slugs, snails, frogs, lizards, snakes and mice. Heavy summer rain may sometimes induce them to feed during the daytime. They are exceptionally resistant to the poison of adders, from which they are normally protected by their sharp spines. When attacked by a predator, the hedgehog rolls itself into a ball and erects its spines. Even so, stoats may sometimes eat them. So many hedgehogs are killed on the roads as a result of their instinctive defensive reactions that selection may now be favouring those individuals that do not roll up, but run away at the approach of danger.

Hibernation is induced by decreasing day length or photoperiod, but is not so continuous as was previously thought to be the case. Hedgehogs tend to wake in very cold weather when they might otherwise be in danger of freezing. In winter, they obtain energy by metabolising the brown fat which has accumulated during late summer. Hedge-hogs do not significantly affect the woodland ecosystem, although they must play their part in the energy flow described in the next chapter.

Rodents and rabbits

Woodland rodents include mice, voles and squirrels. Of these, squirrels are most truly arboreal.

Squirrels The red squirrel probably reached Britain from the continent of Europe by way of a land bridge some 8,000 years ago. It was apparently extinct in Ireland and very scarce in Scotland between the fifteenth and early nineteenth centuries, when extensive reintroductions were made from the continent of Europe. Populations then increased greatly for a while, but dropped drastically again in the mid-1920s. This was probably the result of forest destruction and, possibly, epidemic disease, but at the time the blame was laid on competition with the North American grey squirrel, which had been introduced on a large number of occasions between 1876 and 1930.

Although not a serious pest in its native surroundings, the North American grey squirrel multiplied rapidly when introduced into Britain, spread throughout much of the country and caused considerable damage to young hardwood trees – especially beech and sycamore. Grey squirrels are omnivorous, and do harm by stripping the bark from trees and eating fruit, agricultural crops, eggs and even young birds. In contrast, red squirrels feed predominantly upon tree seeds, especially those of conifers, although beech-mast is also important to them. They are found mainly in coniferous forest, and are now absent from most of England. Squirrels do not hibernate; they build spherical nests, or 'dreys' – in the case of the red squirrel, usually placed in forks of branches near the main trunks of trees; on more exposed branches or in hollow trees in the case of the grey. The grey squirrel spends rather more of its time on the ground than does the red, and is primarily adapted to deciduous woodland and forest. The young of both species are born in spring and summer, and there may be one or two litters of from two to four young per year. Squirrels compete for seeds and nuts with woodland birds; at the same time they increase the amount of food available for birds in winter by disturbing the snow and exposing the leaf litter beneath it.

Mice The mice most plentiful in British woodlands are the yellow-necked mouse, which is found in the woods of southern England and parts of Wales, and the long-tailed field mouse, or wood mouse. Despite their many enemies, which include owls, weasels and stoats, the populations of mice in British woodlands are often surprisingly great, especially when natural predators such as hawks, owls and predatory mustelids have been removed by gamekeepers intent upon raising large numbers of pheasants and partridges. Not only do rodents, especially the bank and short-tailed voles and the long-tailed mouse, eat such large amounts of tree seeds that they inhibit natural forest regeneration, but great damage may be done to young trees by hares and rabbits which eat the bark.

Rabbits Rabbits are no longer classified as rodents, but with hares are given their own group, the 'lagomorphs'. Nevertheless, it is convenient to discuss them here since, like rodents, they gnaw their food. Rabbits become sexually mature at an early age and often begin to breed before they have attained their full size, their litters varying in number from two or three to eight. Although rabbits are notorious for digging extensive burrows, large warrens result only from the efforts of many generations of labour. Since their numbers were so drastically reduced during the 1950s by myxomatosis, the vector of

Woodmouse

Bank vole

which is the rabbit flea, the amount of burrowing has been reduced. The rabbit is, almost exclusively, vegetarian, although sometimes it may eat the odd snail. Its chief food is grass and the tender shoots of furze. Near cultivated land rabbits may damage crops. Burrows are often excavated at the edges of woods growing beside fields. Rabbits favour grassland, especially when this is associated with woods or hedges, which provide cover, but they are not found in coniferous woodland.

Deer

Of the six species of deer now to be found in Britain, three are probably native – the fallow deer may have become extinct and been re-introduced by the Phoenicians or by the Romans – and three have been introduced within the last hundred years or so. The red deer and roe deer are undoubtedly native. Recent introductions are the sika deer, the muntjak and the Chinese water deer. The largest and noblest of all these is the red deer, originally an inhabitant of open deciduous woodland but now frequently to be found on mountains and moorlands in Scotland,

Devonshire and Somerset. The fallow and roe deer are more widely dispersed. The red deer congregates in large herds when living in open country, but in woodlands the groups are smaller. During the breeding season and throughout the winter, the fallow deer may be found in mixed herds of both sexes; at other times, in parties of bucks or does. Roe deer, on the other hand, never form large herds but remain in small family groups.

Deer of all species feed on herbage and the young shoots of trees and shrubs. Roe and fallow deer, in particular, are not content with browsing on the young shoots of trees but may actually kill them by destroying their bark, especially in winter. Fallow deer tend to graze more than the other species, but all feed extensively on acorns and beech-mast in the autumn and winter. Deer play an important part in the woodland ecosystem because of the destruction they cause to young trees and the consequent inhibition of regeneration.

Carnivores

British woodland carnivores include the badger, marten, stoat, weasel and polecat. Otters and the recently introduced mink are

Above Short-tailed vole

Above Yellow-necked mouse

Below Red deer

not true forest animals, although they may be found in woodlands on the banks of lakes and rivers. Badgers have been in Britain since the Pleistocene and are well distributed throughout the country except where they have been exterminated by human beings. They are true woodland animals, dwelling among the trees of oak and beech woods. Their burrows, or 'sets', are, however, to be seen not only in deciduous woodland but also on open pastures. They are most abundant where there is a mixture of the two, but do not extend significantly above the tree-line on mountains.

Badgers are large, strong animals with few enemies other than man. They are omnivorous and feed on young rabbits, hedgehogs, mice, fledgling birds, snakes, lizards, beetles, wasp grubs and other insect larvae. Badgers also eat tree seeds and may, therefore, to some extent be injurious to woodlands. On balance, however, they are probably beneficial because they help to control more harmful animals such as voles and rabbits. For this reason, foresters encourage them, installing special badger gates in the fences so that the animals can roam freely.

The aspiring badger watcher must first find the tell-tale signs of a set, such as discarded bedding straw, deposits of dung, or hairs caught on barbed wire. There will also be disturbed leaves, and shallow pits dug by badgers rooting or scratching the soil for earthworms and beetle larvae. Nearby, there may be footprints on the ground and claw marks on tree trunks. An idea of the size of the badger can be obtained by observing the length of the vertical scoring. This is caused by the badger stretching his limbs to the full extent, while he stands on his back legs and sharpens his claws on the bark. The scores made by badger cubs can sometimes also be seen. It is best to watch for badgers from a concealed spot, down wind from the set, at dusk or dawn. Sometimes they can be tempted to take scraps of meat placed near the

Pine marten

entrances to their holes. A powerful torch may be used without disturbing the animals, so long as it is not pointed directly at them, especially if it is fitted with a red filter. More sophisticated equipment consists of infra-red binoculars used in conjunction with an infra-red torch – or, better still, image intensifier binoculars.

The pine marten was formerly quite common but has been persecuted to such an extent by gamekeepers and fur hunters, and has suffered so much from the loss of its woodland habitat, that it is now rare in Britain and Ireland. Pine martens are solitary, hunting mainly during the night or at dusk and dawn. They are extremely agile and will pursue their prey through the treetops, but travel mostly on the ground. Their diet includes birds, squirrels, mice, voles, eggs, frogs, fish and beetles. The polecat is now confined to Wales and nearby counties, where it frequents lowland wooded country. It is mainly terrestrial, rarely climbing the trees. Its diet is similar to that of the pine marten, but includes more invertebrates.

Stoats and weasels are small, slim carnivores that hunt their prey singly, or in family groups, among dense vegetation – both in the daytime and during the night. They are agile

Young polecat family playing.

climbers, and eat birds and their eggs, mice, voles, rabbits and hares. Of British carnivores, weasels and stoats are by far the most numerous and play the greatest part as top consumers in the woodland food web.

Apart from the omnivorous badger, Britain's two largest carnivores are the red fox and the wild cat. Foxes are widely distributed throughout the countryside, and are preserved by the hunting community. The numbers killed by hunting are small compared with the 50,000 or more foxes destroyed annually by shooting, snaring, trapping and gassing without, apparently, reducing the level of the population. Foxes are nocturnal in habit, and solitary except during the breeding season. The day is spent under shrubs, or in an 'earth' or underground burrow, often acquired from a badger or rabbit. The young number about four or five. They are born in the burrow during the spring, and are weaned within six weeks. They stay with their mother until the autumn. Foxes feed mainly on rodents, but rabbits, birds, beetles, earthworms, eggs,

carrion, fruit and berries are also eaten from time to time.

The wild cat is so similar in appearance to the domestic cat that it may be difficult to distinguish the two in the field. Furthermore, hybrids result when the two species interbreed. The wild cat is extinct in the British Isles, apart from Scotland, but feral domestic cats are to be found everywhere. The wild cat is solitary and nocturnal, an agile climber which hunts mainly on the ground. Its prey consists predominantly of rodents, which are captured by stalking and pouncing, rabbits, birds, frogs and, occasionally, fish. Cats and foxes are the top carnivores of British woodlands.

Bats

From earliest times bats have aroused the imagination and interest of human beings. They are the only mammals capable of true flight, as distinct from gliding, and are usually crepuscular in habit. Many of Britain's bats are woodland species. The greater horseshoe bat, now restricted to south-western England, usually roosts in sheltered, well wooded valleys. It is a heavily built species whose dimensions are only slightly exceeded by those of the noctule, our largest bat. The female bears a single young bat, at the end of June or beginning of July. The lesser horseshoe bat, likewise, frequents mainly wooded country. Its range is less extensive than that of the greater horseshoe bat, but it also occurs in Ireland. It also bears a single young, and has a cry of lower pitch than that of other bats.

The whiskered bat is found in both woodland and open country. Unlike the horseshoes, which roost in colonies, the whiskered bat is usually solitary. It appears earlier in the evening, picking off insects that have settled on foliage, but later catching moths and beetles in flight. Whiskered bats often have their own territories which they patrol throughout the night. The day is spent sheltering in hollow trees, beneath loose bark, in holes in walls, and so on. Again, there is but one young, which is born in June or July. Closely related are Brandt's bat and the rare Leisler's bat, which roosts mainly in tree

Above Head of serotine bat, a species that often roosts in tree holes.

Above Head of noctule bat.
Below Head of long-eared bat.

holes, for preference high in decaying oaks. It, too, occasionally flies during the day, and is not found in Scotland.

The noctule, pipistrelle, barbastelle, Daubenton's bat and long-eared bats are all mainly forest or woodland species. Noctules are colonial, often roosting in large colonies in hollow trees but, occasionally, in smaller holes where they may have to compete with starlings and other birds. The presence of large colonies is often indicated by a thick layer of droppings beneath. Noctules emerge early in the evening and fly high above the trees, sometimes while swallows and swifts are still hunting. They have shrill voices like those of owlets. The pipistrelle is the most widespread and abundant species of bat in Britain, as well as being the smallest. Like the related barbastelle and long-eared bats, it roosts mainly in trees and buildings, sometimes entering caves in cold weather. Large colonies are sometimes found. These bats do not enter their hibernating sites until late in December, and any small bats seen flying during the winter are most likely to be pipistrelles. Like the elusive barbastelle, the pipistrelle often flies low over water, catching its insect prey. Again, the young are usually born singly, in June or July.

Whereas swifts and swallows are the main predators of day-flying insects, during the night their place is taken by woodland bats. The day-active birds locate their prey by sight, the nocturnal bats by echo location. Most bats hibernate in winter when insect food is scarce but some, such as the long-eared bat, may migrate greater or lesser distances – usually, however, only as far as a suitable site for hibernation. Despite the superstitious fancies that surrounded bats in the past, and the persecution to which they were at one time subjected, bats are now popular animals. The movement to protect them and preserve their habitats, spearheaded by British naturalists, is gradually spreading throughout the entire British Isles.

6 Woodland ecology

Ecology is that branch of biological science which deals with the relationships between living organisms and their environments – both physical and biotic. The ecology of woodlands is therefore concerned with the ways in which trees, other plants and animals are affected by climate and soil, and how they interact with one another. In earlier chapters the scene has been set and the *dramatis personae* introduced. In the present chapter the play is in motion and the forest comes alive.

Despite their scientific interest and economic importance, surprisingly little attention has been paid to the study of British woodlands. This may be on account of the size and complexity of woodland communities, the problems incurred in sampling, and the length of time required for trees to grow and mature. British naturalists may be thankful for this because it leaves them a wide-open field in which to develop their interests, with the additional satisfaction of knowing that they will be adding to the store of human understanding. Close co-operation on research projects may be necessary between specialists in different disciplines such as botany, zoology, meteorology, pedology and chemistry: the broad approach of the naturalist is generally more useful, however, than the extreme specialisation which, sadly, afflicts many professional scientists these days.

The ecosystem

The woodland ecosystem is a basic functional unit, including both living organisms and their non-living environment. The former comprise two biotic components: an 'autotrophic' or 'self-nourishing' component which is able to manufacture complex food

substance from simple inorganic chemicals, using the energy of sunlight; and a 'heterotrophic' (which means 'other nourishing') component. This utilises, rearranges and decomposes the complex materials synthesised by the autotrophs. In other words, the trees and other photosynthetic plants as well as nitrogen-fixing bacteria form the bases of the food chains in which decomposing bacteria, fungi and animals play their roles. This may be an oversimplification, but the reader will undoubtedly be asking why on earth such unnecessarily complex terminology was introduced in the first place. The reason is partly to illustrate the way in which professional ecologists approach their subject. They think in terms of energy flow through ecosystems; of producers, consumers and decomposers; of nutrient cycles, food webs and trophic levels; of population dynamics and ecological diversity.

Ecology, the study of the interactions of all living organisms with one another and with their physical environment, would be almost impossible if the field were not subdivided into smaller units or ecosystems, of which temperate woodland is one. Within an ecosystem, the living organisms are grouped according to whether they are autotrophic or heterotrophic – that is, according to their trophic level. The heterotrophs are then subdivided into primary and secondary consumers. In studying the flow of energy between trophic levels, one needs to calculate how much energy enters a given trophic level in a given period of time, such as a year or a season. The amount of this that is utilised in respiration must then be assessed; the amount lost to other trophic levels by grazing,

Above Jay, with nestlings.

Right Woodpigeon

predation, parasitism and decomposition have to be determined. Finally, to balance the budget, allowance must be made for the accumulation of living matter, or 'biomass', within the ecosystem. With this information, it is possible to calculate the efficiency with which the organisms at a particular trophic level use the available energy for growth or reproduction.

The trophic-dynamic model outlined above is regulated by the cycling of various nutrients, shortage of which may impose limitations or thresholds on the ecosystem. Moreover, this is continually affected by season, climate and human activity. No one person could investigate thoroughly every aspect of a woodland ecosystem, but it is important to realise how usefully the findings of one individual study may impinge upon and enlighten the findings of others. Such knowledge may help the investigator to select those points most likely to shed light on the functioning of the ecosystem as a whole.

Energy flow

The vast majority of autotrophs possess the

green pigment chlorophyll which, when provided with radiant energy from the sun, acts as a catalyst for the synthesis of organic materials from water and carbon dioxide. The radiant energy received at the earth's surface is the only source of renewable energy available to living organisms, including man, apart from atomic energy. Since energy can neither be created nor destroyed, its interaction with the woodland ecosystem can, theoretically, be completely accounted for. Some solar radiation heats the air and soil, some provides the energy to evaporate water, and some is incorporated by photosynthesis into the biomass of the vegetation. Of the total radiation reaching the earth's surface, photosynthesis can only utilise energy with wavelengths between 4,000 and 7,000 Angstrom units, and over 15 per cent of this is reflected from the surfaces of the leaves. When allowance is made for this, we find that the theoretical efficiency of photosynthesis is only about 14 per cent at the very most. This does not matter, as sunshine is not rationed. Under natural conditions, even this relatively low figure cannot be attained, presumably because of other limiting factors, such as shortage of water, carbon dioxide and other nutrients, incomplete absorption of light and the release of energy by respiration. Nevertheless, woodland and forest ecosystems are able to attain relatively high levels of energy fixation. Little light penetrates the canopy of tree crowns and a considerable amount of energy is bound up in the wood of the tree trunks – to be released when logs are burned and by forest fires.

Producers, consumers and decomposers

Producers

Biomass is the amount of living material in a given area. Plants are primary producers of biomass, but maximum production is not always correlated with maximum biomass.

There are a number of reasons for this: larger plants, such as trees, contain a lot of non-productive and dead wood; respiratory load increases in larger plants; and there is evidence that older plants, with high biomass, show a decline in photosynthetic efficiency while their rate of respiration remains constant. Primary net production (P) represents the proportion of gross primary production (G) which remains after the energy used in respiration (R) has been accounted for. This can be expressed by the equation $P = G - R$. G and P decline with increasing maturity, while R increases. Enormous variations in rate occur in the different seasons of the year. Moreover, P is reduced by defoliators, such as the larvae of the gypsy moth. These feed on deciduous trees, chiefly eating young oak leaves from the tree crowns. When caterpillars are scarce, there is little loss of spring leaves. Any holes made in the upper leaves allow more light to penetrate to those beneath them – whose photosynthesis is normally limited by the amount of light available – so there is very little loss in net production (P). When partial defoliation occurs, however, less wood is produced and energy is diverted from the production of wood to leaf production; while frass (the excrement of larvae and refuse left behind by boring insects) and dead larvae contribute to the woodland litter, speeding up nutrient cycles in the soil. On balance, therefore, the total production of the ecosystem may be little changed, but the pattern of production and the proportion of wood produced will be altered.

Consumers

In temperate woodland ecosystems, consumers are provided with an immense variety of diets, to which their feeding mechanisms are adapted. In general, however, consumers can be grouped into two or sometimes three trophic levels: primary consumers – herbivores and detritivores; secondary consumers – the predators that feed on them; and tertiary

Above Sparrowhawk

Right Young tawny owl

consumers or 'top carnivores' – which prey on the secondary consumers. There are also parasites, including gall-producing mites and insects, and hyperparasites to complicate the issue.

The numbers of invertebrate animals associated with British woodlands vary according to the number of tree species present, the length of time during which these have been present in the British Isles, and whether or not they are evergreen or coniferous. The taxonomic relatedness, leaf size and height of the trees all contribute significantly but to a lesser degree to the richness of insect species, they support. Figure 24 gives an idea of the numerous categories of insects feeding on woodland trees and the main orders in each category that have a significant impact upon the primary production of forest trees. Figures 25 and 26 illustrate woodland food chains based on leaf-eaters and on vegetarians other than leaf-eaters, respectively.

Decomposers

Woodland decomposers constitute a more heterogeneous collection of organisms than do vegetarian consumers. Among the decomposers are many of the inhabitants of soil and leaf litter that were discussed in Chapters 3 and 4 – bacteria, fungi, protozoans, earthworms, nematodes, woodlice, millipedes, springtails and mites. It is thought that micro-organisms account for as much as 90 per cent of the energy flow through the woodland ecosystem. Their contribution to the production of leaf litter can be measured by harvest methods (see below), in which biomass is sampled after various periods of time. The amount of litter produced can then be related to the entire biomass of wood present, and also to the production of leaves, although the amount falling in any one year is not always the same as the primary production.

Observed differences in the amount of litter production can be attributed to measurable factors including the nutritional status of the soil, the light available for photosynthesis, rainfall and temperature. Other environmental factors which affect all decomposers and soil animals include the acidity of the soil, type, moisture and oxygen content, and the

Above Apple gall on oak.

Above Spangle galls on oak.

Below Robin's pincushion on wild rose.

Below Gall on sycamore.

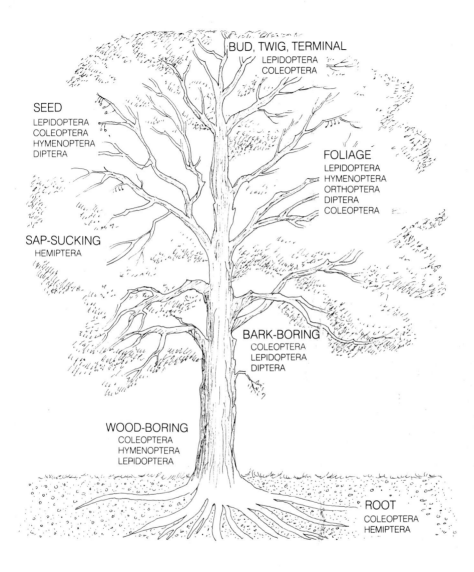

Figure 24 Categories of insect feeding relationships, showing the main orders of insects which have a significant impact upon the production of forest trees.

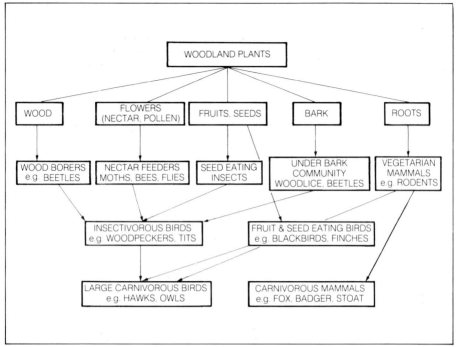

Figure 25 (below) Food chains based on leaf-eaters.

Figure 26 (above) Food chains based on vegetarians other than leaf-eaters.

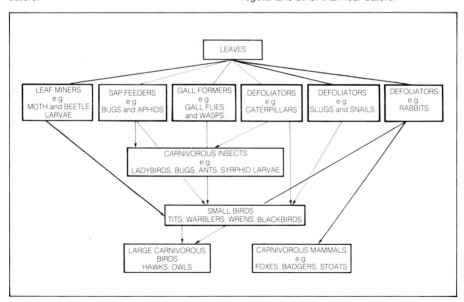

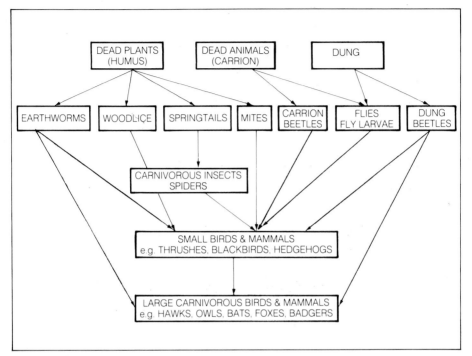

Figure 27   Food chains involving saprophytes and scavengers.

presence and amount of indigestible materials such as tannins. Present techniques do not permit accurate identification and simultaneous measurement of the rate of decay and quantity of humus produced. The food webs that have been studied are inevitably incomplete and the paths of energy flow extremely difficult to follow. Figure 27 illustrates a generalised food chain involving saprophytes and scavengers.

Trophic levels and food webs

Energy flow within and between trophic levels is only one of several ways of considering the structure of the woodland ecosystem. Grazing and the accumulation of biomass are two of the channels along which primary net production (P) can be dissipated.

Energy may pass to decomposers via herbivores and carnivores (the grazing food chain) or directly as litter or detritus via detritivores and carnivores (the detritus food chain). These food chains are usually located in different strata of the ecosystem – the grazing food chain mainly in the canopy of the trees where there is light for primary production, the detritus chain mainly in the leaf litter and soil. There are many other less important food chains in the woodland ecosystem, whose interconnection constitutes the complex food web (Figure 28). Food webs can be expressed as diagrams showing how the different species in a community interact with one another. Of the wealth of interactions which occur, however, only 'trophic' ones that involve energy relationships are of relevance to food chains. Food webs become extremely complicated when parasites are taken into account

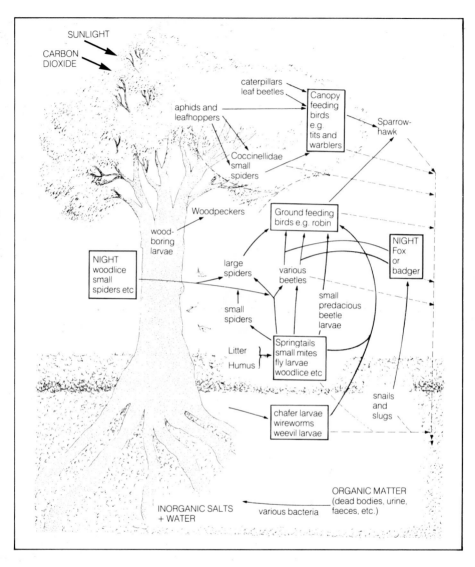

Figure 28   Part of the food web in a British deciduous wood. Arrows show the directions in which food and organic materials move.

but in most cases it is not necessary to include them because they are eaten along with their hosts, plant or animal.

Both detritivores and decomposers may be stratified in the layer of leaf litter on woodland soil. Because carnivores feed on herbivores and on detritivores, they span both strata. On them will feed larger carnivores, and more than three links may be involved in a food chain: herbivore, small carnivore, larger carnivore and top carnivore – the corpses of all of which are broken down to their constituent molecules by the action of decomposers. In Figure 28, for example, herbivores, chafer larvae and wireworms are eaten by ground-feeding birds such as robins, which themselves fall prey to the sparrowhawk. Again, aphids are eaten by small spiders. These, in turn, are eaten by warblers, which, again, may fall prey to the sparrowhawk.

Pyramids of numbers and biomass

At this point it becomes necessary to introduce another ecological concept, that of the 'pyramid of numbers'. Food chains are usually composed of from three to five links. Not only do predators become progressively larger in size at each stage of a food chain, but their numbers decrease. Consequently there is a pyramid of numbers, with very many smaller herbivores or primary consumers at the bottom supporting relatively fewer larger carnivores, the secondary and tertiary consumers, at the apex. This concept is expressed in the Chinese proverb that one hill cannot shelter two tigers. Of course, there are exceptions to this generalisation. For instance, stoats are smaller than the rabbits they eat. Small spiders eat small insects and large spiders catch bigger ones. Nevertheless, they cannot kill goats, nor can tigers catch mice, however hungry they may be. Predators must be large enough to overwhelm and kill their prey or, if the prey is relatively small, they have to be able to catch sufficient for their needs.

There is an optimum size too, for the herbivorous species that form the prey, although this is not so clearly defined. The idea is embodied in another Chinese proverb: large fowl cannot eat small grain. An animal must be big enough to migrate from one feeding ground to another. On the other hand, a large number of small creatures can exploit a limited area much more thoroughly than can a small number of larger forms. Both the sizes of individuals and population numbers are

Fox cubs at play.

adjusted by mutual interactions of this kind.

The information contained within a pyramid of numbers enables an assessment to be made of the number of herbivores supported by a given number of plants, and so on. The difficulty in making comparisons caused by differences in size between different types of producers and consumers can be partially overcome by using the biomass of the various organisms rather than their actual numbers, so that a 'pyramid of biomass' is constructed. Pyramids of numbers and biomass only indicate the amount of material present over a short period of time. The amount of material present at any instant is known as the 'standing crop'. It gives no indication, however, of the total amount of material that is being produced. The standing crop of trees in a mature wood is a measurement of the organic materials that have accumulated over an unknown number of years. Consequently, when studying the functioning of ecosystems it is more useful to measure the rate of production than the standing crop. The information provided by pyramids of numbers and of biomass therefore have their limitations. They can provide information about standing crop, but not about productivity. Some of the objections raised in connection with pyramids of numbers and biomass are overcome by the construction of 'energy pyramids', which show the total amounts of energy used at each trophic level in a square metre over a year. This, at least, provides some quantification of the process of energy flow in the ecosystem.

The pyramids described above apply to herbivores and their predators. When parasitic food webs are considered, inverted pyramids of numbers appear. The primary producers support large numbers of plant parasites, such as nematodes, which are themselves parasitised by bacteria, fungi and Protozoa of even smaller dimensions. Ichneumons, tachinid flies and other small parasites of larger insects, such as grubs and caterpillars, have their own lethal parasites to contend with. These include numerous minute parasitic wasps of different kinds. Such parasites of parasites are known as 'hyperparasites'. Sometimes one parasite may even harbour simultaneously numerous hyper-parasites of different species. Galls result from a complex parasitic interaction between gall-forming insects or mites and their host plants.

The relationships between parasites and their hosts may at one extreme lead to the death of the parasite and at the other to the death of the host. Usually, however, a compromise, intermediate situation occurs so that both parasite and host manage to survive. The antigens released by parasites are counteracted by antibodies produced by the host animal. Plant defences include the presence of distasteful chemicals such as tannins in the leaves, which, to some extent, deter caterpillars and leaf-boring insects. Biological warfare is not a human invention or a contrived term.

Nutrient cycles

Like all plant life, the vegetation of forest and woodland depends upon the circulation of essential nutrients for its growth. These nutrients reach the soil as organic material and then, through the agency of the decomposers, undergo a complex series of changes that break them down to simple chemicals which plants are able to use. The elements required in the largest quantities are hydrogen and oxygen. These are abundant in the terrestrial ecosystem, but shortage of carbon, nitrogen, potassium, calcium, phosphorus, magnesium and sulphur would soon limit plant growth if these essential elements were not continually recycled. Carbon is always present in the atmosphere; but nitrogen, phosphorus and sulphur soon become deficient in soil that is regularly cropped – unless they are replaced by fertilisers. In climax vegetation, however, a stable balanced situation obtains.

The carbon cycle

Plants obtain carbon from atmospheric carbon dioxide, which is present in the air at a concentration of about 300 parts per million. Some carbon is returned directly to the atmosphere by the respiration of the plants themselves, some is excreted by the roots in the form of sugars, amino-acids and other organic compounds, but most is incorporated into the bodies of the plants and animals and is not released until these die and decay (see Figure 29). When the ecosystem is in balance, and organic matter is not accumulating, decomposition must be fast enough to remove the equivalent of all the organic matter being added to the soil. Most rapidly decomposed are carbohydrates, proteins and lipids. Lignin, cellulose and suberin decompose more slowly. These are attacked by bacteria and fungi, and may be eaten by soil animals, of which earthworms and nematodes are among the most important in woodland soils. Material that has already been digested is especially susceptible to attack by microorganisms. Earthworms play an important role, too, by dragging dead leaves into their burrows, where conditions favour decompo-

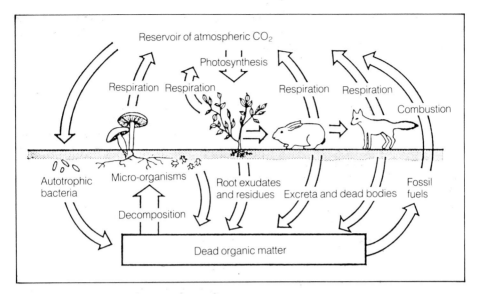

Figure 29 (above)   The carbon cycle.

sition. Complex organic compounds, synthesised by micro-organisms, accumulate to form the humus fraction of the soil, part of which is always slowly decomposing. Plant material eaten by herbivores or omnivorous animals is broken down and returned to the soil in excreta or dead bodies, or released in the form of carbon dioxide during respiration. Many primary consumers are eaten by

Above Sow badger

Right Badger cubs feeding at the base of an elder tree. One of them is scoring the bark of the tree.

Above Long-eared owl

Left Tawny owl

Above Fox

Right Weasel

secondary consumers, and a number of these by top carnivores, so that some of the carbon fixed by plants may pass through the bodies of several animals before it is finally released as carbon dioxide. It has been calculated that earthworms are responsible for about 8 per cent of the total consumption of carbon in English woodlands and, for every hundred millions of earthworms per square kilometre of forest soil, there must be hundreds of billions of nematodes.

Although primary production is, to some extent, restricted by the carbon dioxide content of the atmosphere – and can be increased artificially in glasshouses by increasing the amount of this gas in the air – carbon dioxide is not really a limiting factor on production in the woodland ecosystem. Shortage of nutrients such as phosphates, nitrates, potassium, calcium, sulphur or magnesium may, however, be very important locally. Which of them, if any, actually limits production depends upon the nature of the soil or its 'holding capacity' for nutrients, on the efficiency of decomposition, and on the rate of recycling. In practice, primary production can be measured by harvesting all the plant material in a given area at the beginning of the growing season, drying and weighing it, and repeating the process in a second, exactly comparable, area after a suitable period of time has elapsed. The increase in biomass represents primary production during the period, from which net primary production (P) over a year can be assessed. For an ecosystem in a steady state, the following equation applies:

$$\text{import (I)} + \text{net production (P)} = \text{decomposition (D)} + \text{losses (L)}$$

The nitrogen cycle

The circulation of nitrogen in nature in some ways resembles that of carbon, but there are significant differences. Woodland soils contain much more nitrogen than carbon, but it is in a form that most organisms are unable to utilise. However, many types of soil bacteria and fungi decompose nitrogenous organic compounds into the ammonium salts, while others convert these into nitrates which are taken up by the roots of plants. The nitrifying bacteria which play this essential role in the ecosystem are autotrophic, and obtain all their energy by oxidising ammonium hydroxide to nitrites, and nitrites to nitrates. Some heterotrophic soil organisms can also oxidise ammonium hydroxide to nitrites, but their significance is relatively small. Replenishment of nitrogen in the soil by the biological fixation of atmospheric nitrogen is brought about by symbiotic bacteria that inhabit the root nodules of plants and trees of the clover family Leguminosae. Certain freeliving soil bacteria are also able to fix atmospheric nitrogen. The entire nitrogen cycle is summarised in Figure 30.

The phosphorus and sulphur cycles

Both phosphorus and sulphur are essential constituents of living matter. Soil phosphorus occurs in both organic and inorganic compounds, but most plants can only make use of the latter. Fortunately, many bacteria are able to convert organic phosphorus into inorganic orthophosphate ions. Trees with mycorrhiza can also make use of phosphates, the phosphorus of which is not directly available to other plants.

Like nitrogen, sulphur accumulates in the soil mainly as a constituent of organic compounds which plants cannot absorb. These are, however, converted by the action of micro-organisms into the sulphates that plants do use.

There is considerable interaction between the different substances that limit plant growth in woodlands. In general, the leaf litter produced by deciduous trees has a lower ratio of carbon to nitrogen than that produced by conifers. Furthermore, it decomposes

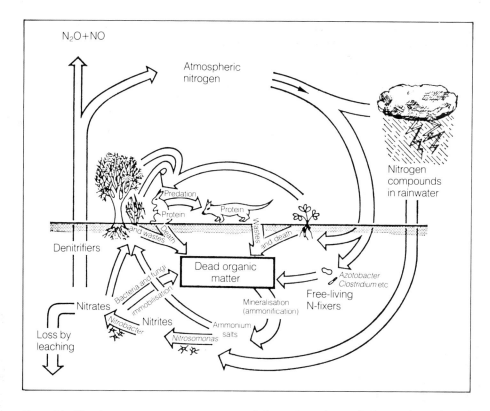

Figure 30 The nitrogen cycle.

faster than do pine needles. Where the parent rock minerals are not too acid, earthworms, millipedes and woodlice contribute to the formation of a mull type of humus. In addition, these animals transport the organic matter from the soil surface to deeper layers of the profile to produce a rendzina or brown forest earth soil type.

Population dynamics

The enormous task of studying energy flow through and within a complex ecosystem restricts the investigator, confining his attentions to individual trophic levels as components of the system. The limitations of this approach inevitably affect the overall study. When numbers of plants or animals are being estimated, samples have to be made, and their statistical significance borne in mind. Life tables must be constructed; biomass, productivity, metabolic activity, photosynthetic efficiency and countless other factors must be evaluated. The situation is further complicated by the fact that some species are common while others are rare, and this situation obtains even when the environment is stable. In addition, in many species population numbers fluctuate markedly from one generation to the next.

Various hypotheses have been proposed to explain the mechanisms by which populations are regulated in nature. So many and so complex are the interactions between organisms and their environments, however, that conclusions reached for one taxonomic group of plants or animals can seldom be

Above Great spotted woodpecker

Left Green woodpecker

lation. Climatic factors, too, may limit the numbers of certain species without actually regulating their populations: they may do this by enhancing intra-specific and inter-specific competition.

Competition

Both plants and animals compete with one another. Competition for light takes place between trees of the same and of different species. When a tree dies or is felled, its place is soon taken by a smaller tree whose growth was previously inhibited by lack of light. Competition between plants also results in stratification of rooting systems. Silver birch and Norway spruce grow very poorly in association with heather. Competition between the seedlings and the heather may be part of the explanation, but another seems to be that heather prevents the development of ectotrophic mycorrhiza in the tree roots. Both inter-specific and intra-specific competition take place among animals also, but intra-specific competition is more intense because it is axiomatic that no two different species have exactly the same requirements.

Cyclical changes

The woodland ecosystem is affected by the two great periodicities of nature, diurnal and seasonal. When darkness falls, the temperature drops and the relative humidity of the atmosphere increases. Photosynthesis ceases, some plant leaves fold and flowers close. Flowers pollinated by nocturnal insects, on the other hand, tend to produce their fragrance at this time. Day-active animals return to their burrows, retreats or roosting places, while nocturnal species emerge to feed, mate and disperse from one place to another.

Changes in the fauna that accompany the transition from day to night provide a fascinating topic for study by the woodland naturalist. Because they lose water rapidly by transpiration in dry air, many cryptozoic animals have to spend the daytime in damp

applied to other groups. Comparison of vertebrate and insect predators, for instance, reveals one interesting difference. The numbers of insect predators in balance with their hosts are several orders of magnitude greater than those of predatory vertebrates and their prey. Food supply sets an ultimate limit to the sizes of some animal populations but often this limit is not reached. In certain cases, a small component of the available food may be essential to the survival of a popu-

Lesser spotted woodpecker

environments where the rigours of terrestrial life are somewhat moderated. It can easily be noticed in the field that the nocturnal emergence of woodlice and of other arthropods, as well as of slugs and snails, is related both to wind speed and to the temperature drop and corresponding rise in relative humidity that occurs at dusk. In order to provide quantitative data in support of the observations, counts should be made during the day and at dusk over periods of several days on a number of tree trunks and areas of bare soil, where the animals can be seen with the aid of a torch. At the same time, temperature and relative humidity should be measured with a whirling hygrometer or electronic apparatus, and wind speed recorded with an anemometer placed as near as possible to the sites of emergence. Very few animals appear on cold nights, which suggests that there is a minimum threshold temperature below which emergence is limited. This appears to vary both seasonally and in different parts of the country, but there is very little factual information on the subject. Work of this nature can well proceed alongside population studies in which capture and recapture methods are employed. Remarkably little is known, too, about the natural enemies of woodlice and other nocturnal arthropods. There is a need for biological observations of predation and all other aspects of natural history from the time of sunset until shortly after nightfall.

Diurnal changes are often integrated with the more obvious seasonal changes that take place throughout the year in the woodland environment. For instance, whereas conifers provide shade throughout the year, woods dominated by beech are shaded only from late April until the end of October. The duration of the shade phase in oak woodlands is from the beginning of May until mid-November, whereas in woods dominated by ash it is only from mid-May until the middle of October. The contrast in illumination between day and night is naturally less in a wood when the leaves of the trees provide shade during the hours of daylight than after these have fallen. Furthermore, oak casts more shade than ash and less than beech, especially when the trees are in open canopy and their branches do not intermingle. These are some of the subjects awaiting investigation by British naturalists.

Observations in very old forests suggest that even climax ecosystems may be susceptible to change. Young trees cease to replace old ones as they die, regeneration of nutrients may lag, and energy flow through the entire ecosystem may be slowing down. The reasons for this, if it really is correct, are not easy to understand. Comparison of the ageing of an ecosystem with individual ageing is scarcely valid, and does not help understanding. It is important to remember that when natural control mechanisms are removed by human interference severe oscillations in population numbers may result. This is the kind of topic about which information might, perhaps, be gained by comparing one wood with another.

Human influences

Neglect

Much of Britain's woodland is neglected. Because of the economic significance of raising large numbers of woodland game birds for shooting, and the destruction by gamekeepers of predatory birds and mammals, large populations of small rodents are encouraged. These eat so many seeds that natural regeneration of the trees is prevented. Financial returns from the renting of shooting rights may far exceed those from timber production. In Britain, the kite, goshawk and honey buzzard have been almost exterminated by gamekeepers and only the sparrowhawk and long-eared owl remain

at all common. Unfortunately, both of these, and especially the sparrowhawk, are threatened by the indirect effect of poisonous chemicals. In recent years, disease and drought have killed millions of trees, while woodlands planted by earlier generations are dying of old age and neglect without being replaced.

Felling and afforestation

Since 1945, Britain has lost between 30 and 50 per cent of its ancient woodlands – those which existed before 1700 – and much of the remainder is threatened by the agricultural policy which subsidises the conversion of forest into agricultural land. Already Britain has a lower proportion of woodland to agricultural land than almost any other European country, and trees are disappearing faster than they are being replanted. Oak, ash, beech and hornbeam are felled to meet demands for increasing food production, while more and more hedgerows are being uprooted for the convenience of mechanised agriculture. Mechanical cutting reduces the chances of young trees becoming established in the hedges that are left. Broadleaved deciduous trees are being replaced by plantations of conifers, which destroys much of their value to wildlife.

The mammal fauna of British woodlands has been profoundly influenced by human activities. The wild boar was exterminated during the seventeenth century, and the wolf disappeared sometime during the following century. In general, wild animals suffer even more from destruction of their environment than they do from direct persecution by human beings. Nevertheless, some woodland mammals have been able to adapt themselves to the destruction of their forest homes, while new woodlands planted in deforested uplands have actually favoured species such as roe deer, fallow deer, foxes, wild cats, polecats and martens. On the other hand, the replacement of indigenous hard wood trees by plantations

Young fallow buck on Cannock Chase.

of alien conifers may tend locally to reduce the number and variety of woodland mammals.

Pollution

Many British forests, like those of Europe and North America, are threatened by acid rain. A by-product of heavy industry, acid rain forms when sulphur dioxide and nitrogen oxide are discharged in huge quantities into the atmosphere by factories which obtain their power from oil and coal. These gases then combine with moisture and oxygen in the air to form rain that not only harms trees but contaminates waterways and erodes the soil. Aerial pollution is a problem that transcends national borders. The Izerskei forests of south-western Poland are polluted by the factories of Czechoslovakia and East Germany. West Germany suffers from acid rain whose constituents emanate from East Germany, Czechoslovakia, France and Britain. Scottish woodlands are polluted from the industrial Midlands and so on. The problem began in the 1960s when high smokestacks were built to carry pollutants away from heavily populated industrial areas. A decade later, it became apparent that these towering chimneys only blew contaminants into outlying forest areas where they can do incalculable harm to the countryside.

Forestry research

The Forestry Commission manages about half of the 2 million hectares of British forest and woodland; the remainder is privately owned. Research is carried out for the benefit of both sectors. Some is of an applied nature, aimed at improving yields of timber and lowering costs of production. Some is more basic. Subjects currently being investigated include genetics and tree improvement, hybridisation between species or between members of the same species from different places, and tree physiology. In particular, research is being directed into the nature of mycorrhizal fungi and their role in the transfer of nutrients between the soil and the fine roots of trees. A major problem in upland forestry is the liability of trees to blow over in strong winds owing to inadequate rooting systems. Methods of cultivation and drainage to encourage the growth of more extensive and deeper roots are being investigated, as well as the aerodynamics of wind passing over and through a forest canopy. With a better understanding of this it may be possible to manipulate the growth of trees so that they are less likely to be blown over. Research on silviculture has demonstrated that growth is increased fourfold or more if trees are planted and supported by shelters consisting of translucent plastic tubes, 9cm square and 1·3m high, supported by thin wooden posts. In addition to increasing growth, such shelters provide protection against damage from rabbits and deer. Much forestry research is also concerned with damage to trees from fungal and insect pests, wood science and processing, harvesting, forest planning and ecological investigations.

Conclusion

The study of woodland ecosystems can follow many interesting paths and byways, but there is no need to elaborate here on the complexity and intricacy of the pattern of interrelationships between woodland flora and fauna.

In this book it has been my aim to outline for the naturalist how the professional ecologist is thinking, so that the naturalist will have a better idea of what information the ecologist requires. Conversely, I hope professional ecologists may be encouraged to make greater use of data assembled by naturalists – for deep knowledge is not acquired from the work of a single individual, but through the synthesis of countless ideas and facts amassed by all kinds of people.

Each original observation or discovery can be a source of wonder and enlightenment – and of a great deal of enjoyment. When shared with others through the medium of natural history societies and through publications such as *Country-Side* and *Naturalist*, it may lead to the formulation of some new concept that enhances the total understanding of nature. There can be few pleasures more rewarding than this.

Further reading

Beirne, B. P., *The Origin and History of the British Fauna* (London, Methuen, 1952).

Bristowe, W. S., *The World of Spiders* (London, Collins, 1958).

Cloudsley-Thompson, J. L., *Microecology* (Institute of Biology, Studies in Biology, No. 6) (London, Edward Arnold, 1967).

Cloudsley-Thompson, J. L., *Spiders, Scorpions, Centipedes and Mites*, 2nd edn (Oxford, Pergamon, 1968).

Edwards, C. A. and Lofty, J. R., *Biology of Earthworms*, 2nd edn (London, Chapman & Hall, 1977).

Elton, C. S., *The Pattern of Animal Communities* (London, Methuen, 1966).

Ford, E. B., *Butterflies* (London, Collins, 1945).

Ford, E. B., *Moths* (London, Collins, 1955).

Freethy, R., *Man and Beast: The Natural and Unnatural History of British Mammals* (Poole, Dorset, Blandford Press, 1983).

Godwin, H., *The History of the British Flora*, 2nd edn (Cambridge, CUP, 1975).

Imms, A. D., *Insect Natural History* (London, Collins, 1947).

Jackson, R. M. and Raw, F., *Life in the Soil* (Institute of Biology, Studies in Biology, No. 2) (London, Edward Arnold, 1966).

Kevan, D. K. McE., *Soil Animals* (London, Witherby, 1962).

Kühnelt, W., *Soil Biology with Special Reference to the Animal Kingdom*, translated by N. Walker (London, Faber, 1961).

Lewis, J. G. E., *The Biology of Centipedes* (Cambridge, CUP, 1981).

Matthews, L. Harrison, *Mammals in the British Isles* (London, Collins, 1982).

Neal, E., *Woodland Ecology*, 2nd edn (London, Heinemann, 1958).

Ovington, J. D., *Woodlands* (London, English Universities Press, 1965).

Packham, J. R. and Harding, D. J. L., *Ecology of Woodland Processes* (London, Edward Arnold, 1982).

Perrins, C., *Birds* (London, Collins, 1974).

Phillipson, J., *Ecological Energetics* (Institute of Biology, Studies in Biology, No. 1) (London, Edward Arnold, 1966).

Reickle, D. E. (ed.), *Analysis of Temperate Forest Ecosystems* (London, Chapman & Hall, 1970).

Sankey, J., *A Guide to Field Biology* (London, Longman, 1958).

Savory, T. H., *Biology of the Cryptozoa* (Watford, Herts., Merrow, 1971).

Schaller, F., *Soil Animals* (Ann Arbor, University of Michigan Press, 1968).

Sutton, S. L., *Woodlice* (London, Ginn, 1972).

Tansley, A. G., *The British Isles and their Vegetation*, 2 vols (London, CUP, 1939).

Turrill, W. B., *British Plant Life* (New Naturalist Series) (London, Collins, 1948).

Unwin, D. M., *Microclimate Measurement for Ecologists* (London, Academic Press, 1980).

Wallwork, J. A., *Ecology of Soil Animals* (London, McGraw-Hill, 1970).

Weygoldt, P., *The Biology of Pseudoscorpions* (Cambridge, Mass., Harvard UP, 1969).

Willis, A. J., *Introduction to Plant Ecology* (London, Allen & Unwin, 1973).

Picture credits

Colour and Black & White Photos

Will Bown: *pages* 56, 66 (both), 87, 88, 97 (both)
Michael Chesworth: *pages* 19 (bottom), 25 (top), 32 (top), 40, 53 (top right), 73, 81, 111, 122
Michael Clark: *pages* 18, 98 (top right), 99, 100, 101 (all), 115 (bottom)
John Clegg: *pages* 82, 106 (top right and bottom left)
Anne Cloudsley: *pages* 11 (top), 14 (top), 23 (both), 27, 53 (top left)
J. L. Cloudsley-Thompson: *pages* 16 (both), 17, 37 (top), 59 (bottom left), 65 (bottom), 79 (top left)
Michael Edwards: frontispiece, *pages* 19 (top right and left), 20–21, 28 (left), 33, 34, 37

(bottom), 39, 41 (both), 42 (bottom), 43, 46, 47 (both), 53 (bottom right and left), 59 (bottom right), 64 (left), 85 (bottom), 92, 94, 103 (bottom), 106 (bottom right), 114 (top), 115 (top)
Ron Freethy: *pages* 28 (right), 32 (bottom), 77, 105 (right)
E. C. M. Haes: *pages* 25 (bottom), 29, 64 (right)
Robert Hare: *page* 67 (top)
John Heap: *pages* 11 (bottom), 26 (top), 30 (both), 42 (top)
Alan W. Heath: *page* 95
Eric and David Hosking: *pages* 118, 119, 120
Robert Howe: *pages* 91, 98 (top left), 114 (bottom)
George E. Hyde: *page* 67 (top)
Dick Jones: *pages* 59 (top), 70

(both), 79 (top right and bottom)
Brian Lee: *pages* 14 (bottom), 15 (both), 26 (bottom), 50 (bottom), 54, 98 (bottom)
Charles Linford: *pages* 103 (top), 105 (left)
Barry Ogden: *pages* 10, 38 (both), 50 (top), 67 (bottom), 106 (top left)
Ian F. Spellerberg: *page* 85 (top)

Cover Photos

Top left: Michael Edwards
Top right: Michael Edwards
Bottom left: Michael Edwards
Bottom right: Michael Chesworth

List of diagrams and drawings

Index

D 1/92